S. Hrg. 113–302

THE DEBT LIMIT

HEARING

BEFORE THE

COMMITTEE ON FINANCE
UNITED STATES SENATE

ONE HUNDRED THIRTEENTH CONGRESS

FIRST SESSION

OCTOBER 10, 2013

Printed for the use of the Committee on Finance

U.S. GOVERNMENT PRINTING OFFICE

88–306—PDF   WASHINGTON : 2013

(II)

CONTENTS

OPENING STATEMENTS

(III)

THE DEBT LIMIT

THURSDAY, OCTOBER 10, 2013

U.S. SENATE,
COMMITTEE ON FINANCE,
Washington, DC.

The hearing was convened, pursuant to notice, at 8:06 a.m., in room SH–216, Hart Senate Office Building, Hon. Max Baucus (chairman of the committee) presiding.

Present: Senators Wyden, Schumer, Stabenow, Cantwell, Nelson, Menendez, Carper, Cardin, Brown, Bennet, Casey, Hatch, Grassley, Crapo, Roberts, Enzi, Isakson, Portman, and Toomey.

Also present: Democratic Staff: Amber Cottle, Staff Director; Mac Campbell, General Counsel; Tom Klouda, Professional Staff Member, Social Security; and John Angell, Senior Advisor. Republican Staff: Chris Campbell, Staff Director; Mark Prater, Deputy Chief of Staff and Chief Tax Counsel; Jeff Wrase, Chief Economist; and Aaron Taylor, Professional Staff Member.

OPENING STATEMENT OF HON. MAX BAUCUS, A U.S. SENATOR FROM MONTANA, CHAIRMAN, COMMITTEE ON FINANCE

The CHAIRMAN. The committee will come to order.

On January 27, 1838, a young State Legislator named Abraham Lincoln spoke before a gathering in Springfield, IL. At the time, America was a deeply divided Nation, and Lincoln warned that the greatest threats to the young democracy were internal.

He said, ''If danger ever reaches us, it must spring up amongst us; it cannot come from abroad. If destruction be our lot, we must ourselves be its author and finisher. As a Nation of freemen, we must live through all time, or die by suicide.''

The actions of the past few weeks, the extremism of a small core of members in the House of Representatives, have crippled Congress and put our Nation on a very perilous path.

For more than 200 years, the United States has been true to its word. It has honored its obligations. It has paid its debts. Yet today, a small group of hardliners is using our economy as a bargaining chip to repeal the Affordable Care Act.

Let me be clear. We are not going to let that happen. The Affordable Care Act is the law of the land. It is not going to be dismantled in this budget fight. The issue is not up for debate.

Our committee wrote the Affordable Care Act. I am always open to this committee working together to strengthen the law to better serve the American people. But as the President said, we cannot negotiate under the threat of default on the Nation's bills. Before any debate, before any deliberation, we need to reopen the govern-

(1)

ment and pay the Nation's bills, no strings attached. Then we need to work together, return to regular order. We must address the Nation's long-term budget challenges working together, including entitlement and tax reform.

But right now, we need to prevent another self-inflicted wound to America's economy. That is what defaulting on the debt is: a self-inflicted wound, with global consequences.

The deadline is fast approaching. In 7 days, the United States Treasury will have exhausted all extraordinary measures to remain under the debt limit. In 7 days, the United States will be at the risk of defaulting on payments. The United States of America, the richest, most powerful Nation in the world, will be forced to look for loose change in the sofa in order to pay its bills.

While the government shutdown has been disruptive, a default would be a financial heart attack. It would have widespread, long-term economic consequences. The national markets are already showing serious signs of stress. The Dow has dropped more than 800 points in the last 3 weeks, and the 1-month Treasury bill rate has risen to its highest level since the 2008 fiscal crisis.

If the debt ceiling is reached, the government would immediately have to slash Federal spending by 20 to 30 percent and drive the Nation back into recession.

The pain will be felt across every sector of society. Social Security and Medicare would be cut, veterans' benefits slashed, funding for highways would be hit. Every government program would be devastated by deep cuts. Families would feel it firsthand with dramatic drops in their retirement savings. Jobs would be lost. Home values would plunge. Interest rates on mortgages and student loans would soar.

Now, some have said we can avoid default by prioritizing U.S. payments, paying bondholders and interest on the debt, but they fail to mention that this scheme would force Treasury to pick and choose which programs to pay, forcing vital programs like Social Security and Medicare to compete for funding. This idea is just irrational.

A default would have a catastrophic impact on the global economy as well. Jim Yong Kim, president of the World Bank, warned that a default would have dire consequences for the world's economy. Christine Lagarde, managing director of the National Monetary Fund, said it is, quote, "mission-critical that the debt limit be resolved as soon as possible."

This is serious. The whole world is watching. Our actions here in the next couple of days will have global implications. We are the most important economy in the world. The dollar is the world's reserve currency. Our Treasury bonds are the backbone of the international financial system. A default would put the global economy in chaos. Of that there is no doubt.

Last week, Treasury warned us that a default would cause a "recession that could echo the events of 2008 or worse." Have people here forgotten what happened in 2008? The collapse of Lehman Brothers set off a financial earthquake. Markets plunged, unemployment surged, America's confidence was shattered to the core. The 2008 crisis upended lives across the country, the aftermath of which can still be felt today.

We cannot let that happen. We have a responsibility to avoid another economic disaster. Our leadership and our resolve will be tested in the coming days. We, all of us here in this room, we have an opportunity to pull America back from the brink.

Earlier this week, I introduced a bill with Leader Reid that would get us past this stalemate. The bill extends the Nation's borrowing authority through the end of 2014, past the midterm elections. It is a clean increase, without any amendments. It simply allows the United States to pay its bills and avoid a catastrophic default. This is only a short-term solution, but it will help pull us back from the edge. It will allow us all here to pause, take a deep breath, and once again try to come together to move forward.

I have been here in the Senate for close to 35 years, in Congress going on 39. I have seen my fair share of partisan fights. But never, in my mind, have I seen Washington so angry, so gridlocked, so broken, and it does not have to be that way.

I know the public might find it hard to believe, but there are some very reasonable people here in Congress. There are many who want to do what is right. There are many who want to work together to conduct the business of our Nation. And I would say to them and to all my colleagues, now is the time. Now is the time for Congress to stop re-fighting old battles. Now is the time for Congress to come together and do what is right for our Nation. And now is the time for Congress to come together, reopen the government, and fulfill America's financial obligations.

I began my remarks with a quote from President Lincoln, and I thought it appropriate to conclude with another one. Lincoln once said, and I quote him, ''I am a firm believer in the people. If given the truth, they can be depended upon to meet any national crisis.'' And that is why we are here today. We need to give the American people the truth, the real facts, and only then, when everyone understands the real risks at hand, the facts and the truth, will we be able to meet this national crisis.

[The prepared statement of Chairman Baucus appears in the appendix.]

The CHAIRMAN. Senator Hatch?

OPENING STATEMENT OF HON. ORRIN G. HATCH, A U.S. SENATOR FROM UTAH

Senator HATCH. Well, thank you, Mr. Chairman. I want to thank you for holding today's hearing on the debt limit. I also want to welcome you, Secretary Lew, to the committee. We appreciate your time and coming at this early time.

During debate over the debt limit increase in 2006, then Senator Obama stated that, ''The fact that we are here today to debate raising America's debt limit is a sign of leadership failure.'' Leadership, he said, ''means that the buck stops here. Instead, Washington is shifting the burden of bad choices today onto the backs of our children and grandchildren. America has a debt problem and a failure of leadership. Americans deserve better.''

Secretary Lew, on the day then-Senator Obama spoke about our debt problem, our gross debt was $8.3 trillion. It is now more than twice that, currently standing at $16.7 trillion. That represents 107 percent of the size of our economy. And, as the Congressional

Budget Office has made clear, this poses large economic and fiscal risks.

During that same 2006 debt limit debate, then-Senator Biden said, ''My vote against the debt limit increase cannot change the fact that we have incurred this debt already and will, no doubt, incur more. It is a statement that I refuse to be associated with the policies that brought us to this point.''

What a difference in attitude there has been since then. Now President Obama and Vice President Biden preside over an administration that tells us that raising the debt limit, in your words, Secretary Lew, ''simply allows us to pay our bills.''

Secretary Lew, you have also publicly stated that only Congress has the power to lift the debt limit. Now, while it is ostensibly true that Congress has the power to raise the debt limit, there will be no increase if the President does not agree. At the same time, despite your public statements to the contrary, it is not true that raising the debt limit has only to do with spending Congress has already approved. This line of argument is based on a premise that Congress makes spending decisions unilaterally and that the Executive Branch plays no role in the process. That premise is simply false. No amount of spending can be enacted without the President signing it into law.

Furthermore, while President Obama's budgets have not been well-received even by Democrats in Congress, the President has traditionally been deeply involved in Congress's efforts to set spending priorities. The administration also issues statements of administration policy and veto threats on spending bills and other pieces of legislation.

Presidents work with Congress all the time to enact their domestic agendas. We all remember how President Obama unveiled and pushed his trillion-dollar stimulus through a Democratic Congress, which he then signed into law.

In addition, this President has made unilateral decisions, with no input from Congress, that have had an impact on Federal spending. For example, there was the decision to delay the employer mandate under Obamacare, which CBO tells us will add an additional $12 billion to our deficit. Congress never voted on the delay. It was a unilateral choice made through rulemaking at the Treasury Department.

So, in short, the commonly repeated notion that questions surrounding spending and the debt limit are Congress's and Congress's alone to answer is, to put it mildly, a case of false advertising on the part of the Obama administration.

There have been several other instances of false advertising from the administration concerning the debt limit. One is the President's claim that non-budget items have never before been attached to the debt limit increase, a claim to which a fact-checker at the *Washington Post* assigned the maximum four Pinocchios, as we have on the chart over here. In fact, of the 53 debt limit increases passed since 1978, under both Republican and Democratic Presidents, only 26 were, quote, ''clean.''

Another is that, in 2011, we entered some sort of a brave new world in which, for the first time in recent history, people were commenting on the inability of Treasury to make timely payment on incoming due obligations. If you would just go back to President Clinton's administration and read some press conferences held by then-Treasury Secretary Rubin, you will see that this claim is also false.

Mr. Chairman, I ask permission to enter a reprint of the press conference in 1995 with then-Treasury Secretary Rubin and then-White House Chief of Staff Leon Panetta that supports this position, along with an associated article from the *New York Times*.

The CHAIRMAN. Without objection.

[The documents referred to appear in the appendix on p. 44.]

Senator HATCH. Now, Secretary Lew, I hope that during today's hearings we do not simply regress into comparative recollections of history. What is at stake is too big for that. The issue we face is yet another debt limit increase. There have been seven debt limit increases since the President came into office, collectively raising the limit from $11.3 trillion to the current $16.7 trillion, a cumulative increase of $5.4 trillion.

When talking about the future increases in the debt limit, all the administration will say is that, one, they want a, quote, "clean" increase, and, two, they refuse to negotiate. Now, we do not know what that means—what they mean by a "clean" increase. We do not even know how much of an increase they want or for how long. Apparently, even making such desires known would constitute a negotiation.

This posture is neither productive nor helpful toward resolving the current impasse over the debt limit. Essentially, what the administration appears to be saying is that it is entirely up to Congress to increase the debt limit and to decide how much and for how long.

This, of course, raises more questions than it answers. For instance, does it mean that if Congress chooses to enact a 2-week clean debt limit increase, the President will sign it? According to the administration's public statements, because Congress is solely responsible for increasing the debt limit, such a hypothetical stopgap would be fine if that is what Congress chose to do. Yet, somehow I do not think that is what the President is looking for when it comes to the debt limit.

In just the past couple of days, the President has expressed willingness to entertain a short-term increase in the limit, which sounds like a willingness to negotiate terms. Sadly, the President's statements are still short on details.

Secretary Lew, the lack of real engagement on the part of the administration is just one of the elements of the current debt limit debate that I find disconcerting. It is also disconcerting to have administration officials, including you, publicly questioning sentiments of Americans and financial market participants and suggesting that people may be too calm, in an apparent effort to whip up uncertainty in the markets.

It is disconcerting that you have suggested that payments of Social Security benefits to retirees and disabled American workers are at risk, especially since you are a trustee of the Social Security Trust Funds. It is disconcerting that administration officials are sounding alarms of emerging risks to financial stability arising from the debt limit and from the debt limit impasse, while, at the same time, the Financial Stability Oversight Council, which you chair, has been silent and refuses to tell the American people how it would respond to these risks.

Finally, it is disconcerting that the administration refuses, in the context of the debt limit, to even have a conversation with anyone concerning our unsustainable entitlement programs, which everyone agrees are the main drivers of our debt. The President has thus far refused to seriously discuss structural entitlement reforms without assurance that he first gets another tax hike.

More often than not, what we hear from the administration on entitlements is a series of disclaimers as to what reform proposals they will no longer consider, and that list seems to get larger every day. The biggest question I have is, if the Obama administration will not negotiate on entitlements in the context of the debt limit, when will they negotiate on entitlements?

Secretary Lew, I will remind you that I have put forth five modest bipartisan reform proposals for our health entitlement spending and personally gave them to the President earlier this year. You have copies of these proposals yourself. Yet, to this day, I have yet to hear a response. I cannot even get mere conversations from the administration about my proposals that I offered in good faith well before the debt limit was even an issue.

Most recently, the Senate Majority Leader has introduced a, quote, ''clean'' debt limit bill, that Senator Baucus referred to, that would increase the debt limit until January 1, 2015, which will likely raise the limit by $1.3 trillion or more. That apparently is the position of the Senate Democratic leadership but is somewhat inconsistent with the President's recent willingness to accept a short-term increase in the debt limit.

As you can see, Secretary Lew, we have a lot to discuss today. My hope is that, during the course of this hearing, we can get a real sense of where the administration wants to go with regard to the debt limit. I also hope that we can get past the arguments that have thus far dominated the administration's rhetoric regarding this issue.

Our Nation's debt is now larger, as a share of our economy, than at any time since the spike-up in World War II. Despite the rhetoric of the administration, our growing debt is not solely the result of decisions made by Congress. It is not all due to the financial crisis, and it is not all the result of tax relief enacted under the Bush administration.

Instead, it is a problem that all of us, both Congress and the executive branch, need to deal with, and the only way to responsibly deal with it is to confront our unsustainable entitlement spending, which will require the administration to do something it is now refusing to do, which is negotiate.

Secretary Lew, as President Obama said in 2006 regarding the debt limit, Americans deserve better.

I want to thank you, Mr. Chairman, and I appreciate you holding this hearing.

[The prepared statement of Senator Hatch appears in the appendix.]

The CHAIRMAN. Thank you, Senator, very much.

Before the Secretary of Treasury begins, I would like to remind members—and I thank you very much for the full attendance—that we have to be very efficient with our questions and our answers. The Secretary has an engagement at 9:30. So I urge us all to respect others as we question so that we all have a chance and the Secretary has a chance to answer our questions.

Mr. Secretary?

STATEMENT OF HON. JACOB J. LEW, SECRETARY, DEPARTMENT OF THE TREASURY, WASHINGTON, DC

Secretary LEW. Thank you, Mr. Chairman. Chairman Baucus, Ranking Member Hatch, and members of the committee, I appreciate the opportunity to appear here today, and I appreciate the invitation to discuss the potential impacts of a failure by Congress to increase the debt limit.

Congress has an important choice to make for the American people, and Congress alone has the power to act to make sure that the full faith and credit of the United States is never called into question. No Congress in 224 years of American history has allowed our country to default, and it is my sincere hope that this Congress will not be the first.

Among the risks that we control, the biggest threat to sustained growth in our economy is a recurrence of manufactured crises in Washington and self-inflicted wounds. Unfortunately, today, we face a manufactured political crisis that is beginning to deliver an unnecessary blow to our economy right at a time when the United States' economy and the American people have painstakingly fought back from the worst recession since the Great Depression.

In addition to the economic costs of the shutdown, the uncertainty around raising the debt limit is beginning to stress financial markets. At our auction of 4-week Treasury bills on Tuesday, the interest rate nearly tripled relative to the prior week's auction, and it reached the highest level since October 2008. And measures of expected volatility in the stock market have risen to the highest levels of the year.

The only way to avoid inflicting further damage to our economy is for Congress to act. I know from my conversations with a wide range of business leaders, representing industries from retail to manufacturing and banking, that this is a paramount concern for them. That is why it is important for Congress to reopen the government, to raise the debt ceiling, and then to work with the President to address our fiscal challenges in a balanced fashion.

Republican and Democratic Presidents and Treasury Secretaries alike have universally understood the importance of protecting one of our most precious assets—the full faith and credit of the United States. President Reagan wrote to Congress in 1983, and I quote: ''This country now possesses the strongest credit in the world. The full consequences of a default or even a serious prospect of default by the United States are impossible to predict and awesome to contemplate. Denigration of the full faith and credit of the United States would have substantial effects on the domestic financial markets and on the value of the dollar at exchange markets.''

If Congress fails to meet its responsibility, it could deeply damage financial markets, the ongoing economic recovery, and the jobs and savings of millions of Americans. I have a responsibility to be transparent with Congress and the American people about these risks, and I think it would be a grave mistake to discount or dismiss them. For these reasons, I have repeatedly urged Congress to take action immediately so we can honor all of our country's past commitments.

The Treasury Department has regularly updated Congress over the course of the last 5 months as new information has become available about when we would exhaust our extraordinary measures. In addition, Treasury has provided information about what our cash balances will be when we exhaust our extraordinary measures. As our forecasts have changed, I have consistently provided updates in order to give Congress the best information about the urgency with which they should act. And last month, I met with the full membership of this committee to discuss these issues.

Treasury continues to project that the extraordinary measures will be exhausted no later than October 17, 2013, at which point the Federal Government will have run out of borrowing authority. At that point, we will be left to meet our country's commitments with only the cash on hand and any incoming revenues, placing our economy in a dangerous position.

If we have insufficient cash on hand, it would be impossible for the United States of America to meet all of its obligations, including Social Security and Medicare benefits, payments to our military and veterans, and contracts with private suppliers, for the first time in our history.

At the same time, we are relying on investors from all over the world to continue to hold U.S. bonds. Every week, we roll over approximately $100 billion in U.S. bills. If U.S. bondholders decided that they wanted to be repaid rather than continuing to roll over their investments, we could unexpectedly dissipate our entire cash balance.

Let me be clear. Trying to time a debt limit increase to the last minute could be very dangerous. If Congress does not act, and the United States suddenly cannot pay its bills, the repercussions would be serious. Raising the debt limit is Congress's responsibility, because Congress and Congress alone is empowered to set the maximum amount the government can borrow to meet its financial obligations.

Some in Congress have suggested that raising the debt limit should be paired with accompanying spending cuts and reforms. I have repeatedly noted that the debt limit has nothing to do with new spending. It has to do with spending the Congress has already approved and bills that have already been incurred. Failing to raise the debt limit would not make these bills disappear. The President remains willing to negotiate over the future direction of fiscal policy, but he will not negotiate over whether the United States should pay its bills.

Certain members of the House and Senate also believe that it is possible to protect our economy by simply paying only the interest on our debts, while stopping or delaying payments on a number of our other legal commitments. How can the United States choose whether to send Social Security checks to seniors or pay benefits to veterans? How can the United States choose whether to provide children with food assistance or meet our obligations to Medicare providers?

The United States should not be put in a position of making such perilous choices for our economy and our citizens. There is no way of knowing the irrevocable damage such an approach would have on our economy and financial markets. Leaders have a responsibility to make our economy stronger, not to create manufactured crises that inflict damage.

In 1987, President Reagan, addressing a debt limit impasse, delivered a message that is applicable to us today: ''This brinkmanship threatens the holders of government bonds and those who rely on Social Security and veterans' benefits. Interest rates would skyrocket, instability would occur in financial markets, and the Federal deficit would soar. The United States has a special responsibility to itself and the world to meet its obligations.''

The very last thing the U.S. economy needs now is a fight over whether we raise the debt ceiling, not when we face serious challenges both domestically and internationally that require our full attention, and not when we know the kind of damage a financial and economic crisis can cause.

Thank you, and I look forward to answering your questions.

[The prepared statement of Secretary Lew appears in the appendix.]

The CHAIRMAN. Thank you, Mr. Secretary.

I would like to focus a little bit on a concept that some suggest as a way out of this problem and which some suggest is feasible, and I disagree with. It is called prioritization. You touched on it.

Could you just briefly tell us what decisions you would have to make as Treasury Secretary, assuming interest was paid on the debt and you then had to choose which other obligations had to be paid?

I know you cannot tell us which ones, nor should you tell us—Social Security, Medicare, military, the farm program, whatnot—but could you just go through the process and describe what the actual legal and administrative problems and consequences would be, and include how much toll that would be?

My understanding is it is about 70 percent to 80 percent of those programs could be paid. And also, what effect would it have on the gross domestic product, that kind of a cut?

Just walk us through the prioritization difficulties, please.

Secretary LEW. Mr. Chairman, let me start by saying what I think should be obvious, that if we do not have enough cash to pay all our bills, we will be failing to meet our obligations and, under any scenario, we will be defaulting on obligations. There is no plan, other than raising the debt limit, that permits us to meet all of our obligations.

When questions are raised about prioritization, the first question is about paying interest and principal on the debt and then, as you said, Mr. Chairman, what else? The legal issues even regarding interest and principal on the debt are complicated.

Let me remind everyone, principal on the debt is not something we pay out of our cash flow of revenues. Principal on the debt is something that is a function of the markets rolling over. So there is a question of what we can do as a government and how the markets function when the government is failing to pay all of its bills. We have never been there, and I think anyone who suggests they know exactly what that means would be projecting, after 224 years of the history of paying all of our bills, what happens if we stop paying all of our bills.

Mr. Chairman, I do not know how you could possibly choose between Social Security and veterans' benefits, between Medicare and food assistance. These are obligations we have made.

We would not have the money to necessarily pay our troops in full. We would not have the money to pay our veterans their benefits in full. Our systems were not designed to not pay our bills. Our systems were all designed to pay our bills.

The legal issues are many. I do not know how you could make the decisions. I do not think the legal authorities are clear at all, and I do not think the administrative process would permit the system to work.

We write, roughly, 80 million checks a month. The systems are automated to pay, because, for 224 years, the policy of Congress and every President has been, we pay our bills. You cannot go into those systems and easily make them pay some things and not other things. They were not designed that way, because it was never the policy of this government to be in the position that we would have to be in if we could not pay all our bills.

The CHAIRMAN. Now, if we were to prioritize, it is my understanding, as well, that you know, to some degree, what your outpay obligations are—for example, there is a big Social Security payment due October 23rd, interest on the debt the 1st, and at the end of the month, this month, a major Medicare payment, and other bills due.

But on the other hand, we know that the revenue is a little bit sketchy, it is lumpy. It comes in in unanticipated amounts.

Could you go over that a little bit, please?

Secretary LEW. Well, that is very much the case, Mr. Chairman. We have estimates. If these estimates are wrong, then there is the real risk of miscalculation. And I would just note, even in the period of time that I have been keeping Congress informed, we have seen swings in the normal course of things of $20 billion in terms of our estimate of what the cash on hand would be. And that is not because anyone did anything wrong; it is because quarterly tax receipts were not exactly where they were estimated to be.

I would also remind everyone that we are now in an unusual position with the government shut down. That is having economic consequences that we are just beginning to understand.

All of the revenue projections that we have based our analysis on were based on a world where the government was functioning and where all of the services that relate to government activity were happening. So they did not take into account any layoffs that might occur. It did not account for any reduction in payroll or payroll taxes.

So I have to assume that the estimates from before shutdown are likely not to be an accurate predictor of exactly where we are.

The CHAIRMAN. How do you reprogram computers?

Secretary LEW. Well, Mr. Chairman, I have to tell you, I do not believe there is a way to pick and choose on a broad basis. The system was not designed to be turned off selectively.

So anyone who thinks that it can be done just does not know the architecture of our multiple payment systems, which are very complex. They were designed properly to pay our bills. They were not designed to not pay our bills.

The CHAIRMAN. In short, prioritization just does not work.

Secretary LEW. I think prioritization is just default by another name. It is just saying that we will default on some subset of our obligations. But we are still—by definition, if we do not have enough money to pay all of our bills, we will be in default on our obligations.

The CHAIRMAN. Thank you.

Senator Hatch?

Senator HATCH. Thank you, Mr. Chairman.

Secretary Lew, I want to be clear about the administration's position on the debt limit. As I understand it, the position is that the President will only accept a so-called ''clean'' debt limit hike with no other accompanying policy or fiscal considerations attached to it.

I have asked you repeatedly how much of a debt limit increase you would like and for how long, and you have responded that it is up to Congress.

Now, I believe that the administration's position is unfortunate, because it is clear that we have a debt problem and that the fundamental driver of our debt is unsustainable spending in our entitlement programs.

I believe we can and should use this as an opportunity to address these problems, and I have personally, as I mentioned, offered five modest bipartisan proposals on entitlement reform to the President earlier this year. You have received copies. Unfortunately, I have heard no responses to those, and I sincerely did that. Nevertheless, the administration is entitled to its opinions and positions.

So I just want to be clear concerning the debt limit. As long as there is nothing attached to a debt limit increase, the administration will say nothing more about it, including its preferred outcomes in terms of how much of an increase and for how long.

Is my understanding correct, or do you wish to give me your preferences about how big of a debt limit increase you would like to have and for how long you would like it, so that at least we can begin discussions and negotiations on this particular issue?

Secretary LEW. Senator, you and I have discussed this a number of times, and we have corresponded a number of times. I wrote to you just last week, a few days ago, stating what our view is. Our view is that this economy would benefit from more certainty and less brinkmanship. So the longer the period of time is, the better for the economy. It is really Congress's decision how often it wants to vote on the debt limit.

I believe that more certainty is better. I think the Senate leader and the chairman have put forward a proposal——

Senator HATCH. Mr. Secretary, all I am asking is, how much do you want and for how long? I mean, those are two simple questions. How much do you want us to raise it and for how long?

Secretary LEW. Senator, the question of how long is one I think I am answering as clearly as I can. The longest that Congress is prepared to extend it for is the best. The President tried to be clear in his statements in recent days that if Congress passes something shorter, he was open to—he is not looking for there to be a crisis here, but Congress went right back dealing with it. So the better solution is to go longer.

So we tried to be very clear, and everyone knows the numbers that are associated with different periods of time.

Senator HATCH. Well, it is not clear to me.

Now, Secretary Lew, the recent long-term outlook from the non-partisan Congressional Budget Office makes a number of things abundantly clear.

First, between 2009 and 2012, the Federal Government recorded the largest deficit since 1946, causing Federal debt to soar, as a share of our economy, to an amount higher than at any point in U.S. history, except a brief period during World War II. Gross debt now stands at 107 percent of our GDP.

Second, our debt path is unsustainable, threatening to bring us to this fiscal crisis.

Third, the root of our spending problem is the government's major health care programs. That includes not just Obamacare, but Medicaid and Medicare as well, and others.

Fourth, trust funds in Social Security and health entitlement programs face exhaustion. Yet, when it comes to negotiating solutions to our entitlement spending problems, all I hear from the administration is that negotiations can only proceed if, first, the President is guaranteed yet another tax hike, or if the only spending restraint we have enacted thus far is turned off.

Now, when it comes to so much as even discussing solutions to our entitlement spending problem, all I hear is that negotiations can only proceed if, first, we pass a clean continuing resolution and a clean debt limit increase.

Now, what does it take beyond a guarantee to the President and congressional Democrats that they first get yet another tax hike or that the sequester be undone to get the administration to the table to talk about entitlement reforms such as the ones I have proposed and which to date have been met with total silence from the administration?

Furthermore, is it reasonable to say that there can be no negotiations unless there is another tax hike, when we know, to this very day, that disabled American workers face a benefit cut of 20 percent or more under current law when the Disability Trust Fund is exhausted in 2016 or earlier?

Secretary LEW. Senator, I think the record is clear that the President has negotiated, has wanted to negotiate, and remains anxious to negotiate, on a bipartisan basis to have a fair and balanced approach to dealing with our fiscal problems.

Senator HATCH. It is not clear to me.

Secretary LEW. He has been on the verge of agreements twice, until, frankly, it was not acceptable to Republicans in Congress. He was prepared to do very hard things. He was ready to have an agreement twice, in 2011 and at the end of last year.

He put in his budget very tough policies, policies that many of the Democrats on this committee find very challenging, because he wanted to make clear he was looking for a balanced approach to entitlement reform and tax reform to settle our fiscal matters in a sensible way for the medium and long term.

So I think the President's record on being willing to negotiate is clear.

I would just make one comment——

The CHAIRMAN. Briefly.

Secretary LEW [continuing]. Very briefly—on the trajectory of our deficit. I would just note that, when the President took office in January 2009, we were in the middle of the worst recession since the Great Depression, we were in the middle of two wars, and we had a deficit that was 9 percent of our economy. We have cut that in half. We are making progress.

We have more to do, but I do not think it is fair to say that we are in the same place we were. We have made tremendous progress.

The CHAIRMAN. Senator Wyden?

Senator WYDEN. Thank you, Mr. Chairman.

Mr. Lew, it seems to me, in the event of a default or a near-default, the dominos are going to fall fast and hard, and those hit early on will be older people who depend on their own retirement savings to get by. These are the older people who saw much of their life savings evaporate during the recession, and they are struggling just to get those private savings, in effect, back to the water line, back to where they are.

Be as specific as you can with respect to what default or near-default would mean for those seniors who depend on their private savings.

Secretary LEW. Senator Wyden, I can only begin to imagine what it would mean to a retired American who relies on Social Security as their major or sole source of income if we had to tell them their check was going to be late.

I remember my late mother lived on her Social Security check. Many of us have relatives who live on their Social Security check. If the check did not come, if they did not have the ability to call someone who could help them out, they were in trouble.

So anyone who thinks that anything short of default would be fine, has never experienced what it means to live on Social Security.

In terms of Medicare——

Senator WYDEN. With private savings especially, Mr. Secretary— I share your view about those others, but I think the public has heard and you have given some comments with respect to mortgages, but I am concerned about those retirees and their private savings as well.

Secretary LEW. Retirees saw their private—well, let us talk not just about retirees, because workers have their savings at stake as well. The effect is the same, it is just more immediate for retirees. Retirees have no time to catch up.

We saw during the financial crisis that people's retirement assets fell quite dramatically in value. It reduced what retirees had to live on. It caused anxiety among working people about how they were going to make up for the ground that they lost.

We are now in place where, because of the resilience of the American people, the recovery in the American economy, the good policy decisions made by Congress and the Federal Reserve Board, we are in a better place. We have a lot of work to do, but I think you can see from the economy that people are beginning to feel that the economy is moving in the right direction.

Now, if you create a crisis that causes assets to shrink in value, for retirees, they do not have a lot of time to catch up. So, even if it all rights itself over a period of time, for those retirees, they are in a pretty bad spot. So I think it is very unfair to have manufactured crises that have a real life impact on working Americans and retirees who ought to have to worry only about market risks, not government policy risks.

Senator WYDEN. Let me ask you about the effect of default on the deficit. Now, we know that budget sequestration has not exactly been an ideal instrument, not exactly perfectly targeted for driving down the budget deficit. But it has produced budget savings that actually accrue to the benefit of the American taxpayer.

In the event of a default or near-default, is it fair to say that some of those budget savings would be eaten up to pay higher interest costs, a substantial amount of which would go to foreign governments and to other foreign creditors?

Secretary LEW. Well, Senator, we have seen just this week that, for the bills that mature at the end of October, the rates have almost tripled over the last week. We still have access to the credit markets, but it is more expensive, and for no reason. It could be resolved by just settling this issue and making it clear that the debt limit will not be breached and we will not have any problems.

Senator WYDEN. What is troubling to me is, after the American taxpayer has gone through something of a painful process and you see these savings, the results of a default would produce higher interest payments and, in effect, transfer American wealth from our taxpayers, and some of that would go to foreign creditors.

Secretary LEW. And, Senator, I would just add that higher interest rates also flow through the economy in terms of higher mortgage rates and higher student loan interest rates. So the costs have multiple levels of impact on real people.

Senator WYDEN. Thank you, Mr. Chairman.

The CHAIRMAN. Thank you, Senator.

Senator Grassley?

Senator GRASSLEY. Secretary Lew, Majority Leader Reid's clean debt limit increase into the beginning of 2015 would likely be an increase of around $1.3 trillion. But my understanding of the administration's position is that it is leaving the debt limit increase entirely up to Congress, that you will not negotiate, you require a clean debt limit increase, and you will say nothing about your negotiating preferences regarding how long or how much of a debt limit increase is desired.

With that being the case, if Majority Leader Reid's clean debt limit bill were amended to raise the limit for 1 month and the amended bill were passed through Congress, then the President would sign it, I assume. Is that correct?

Secretary LEW. Well, Senator, I would have to, obviously, see a bill, and the President would have to look at it to say what he would not sign. But the President made clear that he thinks dealing with this for a longer period of time would be good for the economy, but he did not rule out doing something shorter, if that is what Congress does.

I think we have been very clear about what we think the right thing to do is.

Senator GRASSLEY. Both you and President Obama have repeated the talking point that negotiating deficit reduction policies on the debt ceiling increase is unprecedented. The debt limit has been used in the past as a means to enact deficit reduction policies.

I quote the Congressional Research Service: ''Since 1978, Congress has voted to raise the debt ceiling 53 times. In 27 of those, or 51 percent, the debt limit increase was tied to other reforms.''

I assume you are aware that more often than not, the debt ceiling is raised with other policy or reforms. If you are so aware of that history, why do you and President Obama continue to use the talking point that negotiating on a debt limit bill is unprecedented when the facts demonstrate otherwise?

Secretary LEW. Well, Senator, I do not think that is an accurate version of history and certainly not what I recall, having lived through many of the budget debates over the last 35 years.

If you look at the last nine budget agreements, only three of them have involved the debt limit. So it is not the case that most budget agreements involve the debt limit. If you look at the budget agreements that did not involve the debt limit, in several of them, the debt limit was just added onto a bill. It was not driving the debate.

What I think changed in 2011 was that the affirmative case was made in 2011 that if a certain faction—and I am not saying it is the people in this room—but if a certain faction in the House did not get their way, they would prefer default over a compromise that they found unsatisfactory. That is different. It is just different.

We cannot have the debt limit be something that is a threat to the economy unless policy concessions are made. That is not how our democratic system works. A minority cannot do that.

Senator GRASSLEY. Secretary Lew, before I go on to my next question, at least you cannot say that it is unprecedented to have negotiations and reforms tied to a debt increase.

Secretary LEW. I have never said it is unprecedented for debt increases to be tied to actions. But debt increase has always been a hard vote. Since 1917, this country has been working to try to turn it into a more ministerial vote. Congress used to have to vote on every bond issue. The debt limit was put in place to reduce the number of times Congress had to vote on debt.

In the 1970s, when I was working for the House Speaker, we tried to turn it into an automatic vote so there would not have to be a vote on the debt limit. Just 2 years ago, Senator McConnell put in a mechanism to try to make it easier to vote on the debt limit. It has always been a hard vote.

The question is, is it going to be used as a threat to the economy, and that cannot be.

Senator GRASSLEY. Secretary Lew, the President has made clear that if we pass a clean continuing resolution and a clean debt limit extension, he is ready to negotiate. Where we need to negotiate is obvious. If you look at long-term projections, spending on our health care entitlements demands our attention.

In the next 25 years, spending on Medicare and Medicaid as a percentage of GDP is projected to double, nearly. Now, if I ask you if the President is willing to negotiate on health care entitlements—I think you have already mentioned what the President put in his budget—you are probably going to cite the President's budget. You have already done that.

I do not consider that negotiation. I consider it a restatement of your position. Negotiation means you are willing to give serious consideration to the other side's ideas.

Senator Hatch has made numerous, serious proposals on health care entitlements. I am told that the message of the 2012 election was that Democrats no longer have to negotiate on health issues.

Can you convince me that that is wrong?

The CHAIRMAN. Senator Schumer?

I am sorry, Senator.

Senator GRASSLEY. Can he answer this question?

The CHAIRMAN. In about 10 seconds.

Secretary LEW. Senator, I think the President's budget does reflect his openness to serious entitlement reform. He has been willing to work on a bipartisan basis to do things that are unpopular on the Democratic side, and he is just looking for a partner to work with who is willing to have some give-and-take, not just one way.

The CHAIRMAN. Senator Schumer?

Senator SCHUMER. Thank you, Mr. Chairman.

And thank you for coming, Secretary Lew. This hearing is much needed. I think if it has a purpose, it is to deal with the debt ceiling deniers. The debt ceiling deniers try to claim that default will not be a big deal. Middle-class families will not be hurt. We can just pick and choose which bills to pay. Prioritization, they call it.

Well, the debt ceiling deniers need a dose of debt ceiling reality, and you have given them that today. Basically, you have said, I think in just about these words, you said prioritization is default by another name. And prioritization is extremely difficult, as you have said.

Do we pay foreign debts or veterans' benefits? Do we make sure Social Security benefits go out or pay Medicare? Do we pay for education? Do we pay for our troops?

The American people do not want that. They would certainly want us to just pass a clean debt ceiling bill and avoid those awful choices.

By the way, one of these debt ceiling deniers, I read in the *New York Times*, a Congressman named Brown, has also said that much of what he learned in medical school was lies. They came from, in his words, "the pits of hell." If we are letting people like this lead us, God save America.

Now, I would like to deal with the second issue, which is the timing. In my view, we are like a blindfolded man walking toward a cliff, and, if we keep walking in that direction, very soon we will fall off. We may fall off on October 16th, we may fall off on October

17th, we may fall off on October 25th or November 1st, but we will fall off.

And the most interesting part—the most important point about this—is, we do not know which day we will fall off. The markets are somewhat mystical. They could, even a day or two before October 17th, come to the view the U.S. is going to default, anticipate that, Treasuries go down in value, interest rates go up, much of our financial system freezes, and we are back where we were in 2008 when AIG failed.

So I just want to ask you this question to be clear. Is there not a risk almost every single day, starting around October 17th, even perhaps a day or two earlier and getting worse, that we cannot tell exactly when each day after that we will not have enough money to pay our bills and default could occur, even if you laid out the most meticulous plan in the world?

Secretary LEW. Senator Schumer, I have been trying to be as transparent as possible for several months, because I very much fear that a miscalculation is something that could lead to an unintended, but very severe, consequence.

Since August, I have been very clear, we are already in overtime. We hit the debt limit in May. We have been using extraordinary measures. We call them extraordinary measures, but everyone now assumes that they are infinite. They are not infinite.

I warned in August that we are going to run out of extraordinary measures sometime in the middle of October, and I even went the step further, which mostly has never been done, and said we are going to have roughly $50 billion in cash.

A month later, based on the year-end tax receipts and expenditures, I updated it, and I said no later than October 17th we would run out of borrowing capacity, and, instead of $50 billion, we would have roughly $30 billion.

Now, I think that should indicate that what I said in each of these correspondences is true. It is impossible to predict with accuracy. We are talking about enormous variations in day-to-day expenses and in economic activity which generates tax revenues. So it is impossible to predict with accuracy.

It is typical to keep roughly $50 billion in reserve at all times just as a cushion against the unknown. So, when you talk about having less than $50 billion and drawing it down, it is a dangerous place to be. That is why Congress needs to act to raise the debt limit sooner rather than later.

Senator SCHUMER. One way to avoid a potential cataclysm is to pass a clean debt ceiling increase now, not delay and say, well, we can wait until the eve of the 17th or the 19th or October 31st. Is that right?

Secretary LEW. Well, I must say there is a parlor sport in Washington of, when is the last minute? You cannot do that with the debt limit. With the debt limit, if you look for the last minute and you make a mistake, you have done serious damage to the U.S. economy, to the world economy. It is just not responsible. It is reckless.

Senator SCHUMER. So would you agree that my analogy—blindfolded man walking toward a cliff, and we do not know exactly what date he will fall off, but if he keeps walking, he will—is pretty accurate?

Secretary LEW. I have tried to describe it in my own words.

Senator SCHUMER. Thank you, Mr. Chairman.

The CHAIRMAN. Thank you, Senator.

Senator Crapo?

Senator CRAPO. Thank you.

Secretary Lew, you indicated in your beginning remarks that we face a terrible threat to the economy from a manufactured crisis. And I understand the fact that the issue of whether the Federal Government's borrowing limit should be raised is problematic and creates serious concerns with regard to our economy.

But the fact is that we do face a debt crisis, not a—well, I guess it is manufactured over decades now, but we face a real debt crisis. And, as we hear in the discussion about whether the United States is going to lose its good faith and credit ultimately or go into default, I think the real crisis is that default, the one that we are screaming toward because of our refusal to engage, as a country—Congress and the President—with regard to reforming our failed entitlement system, reforming our failed tax policy in this country, and dealing with the real debt crisis that we face.

I think Senator Schumer's comment about the blind man walking toward the cliff is even more appropriate with regard to the debt crisis that we face with a $16-trillion, almost now $17-trillion debt.

So my question to you is, do you not believe that the long-term trajectory of our debt gives our economy a greater threat and gives investors even more concern in terms of their confidence about the ability of the United States to avoid default?

Secretary LEW. Senator, we clearly have long-term challenges, but I think the financial markets—when you talk to financial lead policymakers around the world, they actually see that we have made a lot of progress in the last few years. We have more to do in terms of entitlement reform and tax reform, but we have taken a deficit that was 9 percent of GDP, and we have cut it in half to 4 percent of GDP.

If anything, we are getting criticized around the world for having done too much deficit reduction too fast, because they want more growth.

Senator CRAPO. But, Mr. Secretary, you mentioned——

Secretary LEW. I very much agree that we should be dealing on a bipartisan basis with—and you and I have talked about this—sensible, balanced approaches for medium- and long-term reforms, and I would love to be engaged in that conversation——

Senator CRAPO. But the very progress——

Secretary LEW [continuing]. But it is not the crisis that we are talking about.

Senator CRAPO. The very progress you are talking about occurred as a result of significant tax increases and a debt ceiling compromise that was reached with the Budget Control Act.

The fact is that we have not dealt—and in that compromise, we dealt with discretionary spending almost entirely. We have not dealt with entitlements, which the administration seems to say are off the table, and now we have yet even more demands for greater tax hikes. And that is what the negotiations that we want to engage in are all about.

Secretary LEW. Senator, the President has engaged on multiple occasions, and I have been part of those negotiations. We very much believe that a balanced approach, where you do entitlement reform and tax reform, would be good for the country.

We tried in 2011, we tried in 2012. We are ready to try again. The President said, when we take away the threat of economic disaster, he is ready to engage. If I heard him correctly in his press conference the other day, he said he would pay for dinner.

So he is willing to talk and wants to talk, but it cannot be that it is with the U.S. economy being threatened if one small part of Congress does not get its way.

Senator CRAPO. So, we need another $1 trillion or more of debt authorized before we can even discuss whether to start reforming entitlements, whether to start reforming the tax code?

Secretary LEW. Senator, what we believe is, the government needs to open. Congress needs to open the government, and Congress needs to make it possible to pay our bills, and we need to engage. And we are ready to do that.

Senator CRAPO. Well, just to conclude my questioning, then. Back to the issue of our long-term debt and the threat that it poses to our economy, are you telling me that those fears have now been allayed?

Secretary LEW. No, Senator. What I tried to say is, and I hope I was not confusing, there is a challenge to deal with in the medium and the long term. It is not the same as a crisis, which is what happens if you fail to act on the debt limit in the next short period of time.

I would very much like to do it sooner rather than later. I think it is better for the country. It would have been better for the country if we had been able to complete the negotiation where the President and the Speaker were very close, until House Republicans said they would not vote for it.

We would love to be in a place where we were talking about a sensible alternative to these mindless across-the-board cuts. We have been very clear about that. But it cannot be with the threat that the government is shut down and we are going to default on our bills. That is not the way to engage in the kind of bipartisan negotiations that need to happen.

The CHAIRMAN. Senator Cantwell?

Senator CANTWELL. Thank you.

Secretary Lew, thank you for your testimony about how you think that the serious prospects and uncertainty to the market are happening right now. That is my question to you, because everybody is talking about default as if that is the triggering point, and I think your testimony lays out that this moment could happen at any time.

The reason I brought this chart is that everyone thinks Treasury notes—if you are not involved in the financial markets or have not been in the business community—are some mysterious thing. But this chart shows that Treasuries are held not only in the U.S. by businesses, but in Europe and China, and they are significant. It is a network. It is as complicated and complex as just about anything around when it comes to all the individuals who are involved. It is not, as one of our colleagues said, picking up the phone and calling Wall Street and telling them to settle down.

I just went on the web and said, ''what about Treasuries.'' If you just Google ''Treasuries,'' what comes up is 'the most important market indicator,' way more important than the Dow and the S&P. It is an important number in the economy because of the interest rates being pegged off of its interest rate.

So here we are now, basically almost, talking the interest rate up with the talk in DC. And in the last 48 hours—I wish I could print out this chart, because we have seen a spike, a dramatic spike from .03 percent to .297 percent. That is more than a doubling in 48 hours.

So my question is, if the interest rate on Treasuries doubles in the next 48 hours again, are we not already to that tipping point?

Secretary LEW. Senator, I have been trying to be very careful and just report what has happened. I am not going to predict what markets will do. I do think that if you look from last week to this week, a tripling of interest rates on short-term bills is not a good thing.

We have seen stability in the long-term bond markets, but markets are delicate things, and I do not know how markets will translate one day's news, one day's action, into discomfort.

What I do know is that every week we roll over $100 billion of Treasury bills, and that relies on the market being open and willing to function. And I just think everyone has to remember that it is not just the interest, it is also the principal. The markets have to keep working.

Senator CANTWELL. I think the thing that people are missing here in DC is that everybody is at risk in the U.S. economy. It is not just what you just explained, but everybody at home.

Last time we had this discussion about whether we were going to default or not, the stock market dropped 20 percent. So we could have this same discussion, and then by Friday or Monday, you could see—in fact, one of my constituents who is an analyst said you could see as much as a 25-percent drop in the stock market, just triggered off of Treasuries. So we do not have to go to default—just the talk of default is causing the level of uncertainty that we are all trying to avoid.

Secretary LEW. Well, Senator, that is what we saw in 2011. In 2011, we had an 11th-hour agreement, and we avoided seeing what happens when you cross the line. But we had the damage. We had the drop in the market. We had the higher interest rate costs. We also saw for the first time a downgrade in the U.S. credit rating.

So that is what happened when we did not cross the line. I do not think anyone should want to test what happens when we cross the line. We are seeing, with the government shutdown, that every day new things are coming out that are really bad. People who thought it was okay to shut down the government are now rushing to open up one piece or another at a time.

It would be reckless to see what happens when you cross the line and do not pay America's bills.

Senator CANTWELL. I think what we are doing right now is reckless. So I hope our colleagues—I hope we will come together. Thank you.

Thank you, Mr. Chairman.

The CHAIRMAN. Thank you, Senator.

Senator Roberts?

Senator ROBERTS. Thank you, Mr. Chairman.

I do not think we have a blindfold on and are walking toward a cliff. I think we are walking toward a cliff with our eyes wide open, and that is the problem.

All this talk about self-inflicted wounds—it was not a self-inflicted wound when we raised the debt limit and we also achieved the Gramm-Rudman-Hollings Act, the Social Security amendments, the Balanced Budget Act, the Budget Control Act, and I could go on and on with the fact sheet here that has been referred to by other Senators.

I think it is down to a willingness to really negotiate. The President has said over and over and over again that he will not negotiate, but I do not think that is true. There is a meeting as we speak with the Republican leadership. Yesterday he met with Democrats.

My question to you is, you have been briefed on the agenda of this meeting with regard to the time that the President would prefer with regard to an extension of the debt limit and the agenda, and, more especially, I am talking about sequester flexibility with Appropriations Committee oversight, the repeal of the medical device tax, the restoration of a 40-hour work week to the ACA as opposed to the 30-hour work week that is causing all the problems, and perhaps even a decision or at least a time frame on a decision on the Keystone Pipeline.

There is a long list that all of us have that we have been talking about, more especially, Senator Crapo was asking specific questions on entitlement reform, and that is the real cliff with our eyes wide open that I think that we are walking toward.

I would only opine to you, sir, that the reason why this is so tough is, the American people get this—maybe not on the shutdown, although there has been a lot of debate back and forth, but they sure get this on the debt limit; 52 percent do not want any increase in the debt limit. They get it.

They look at this as their own family budget, and they understand this. Seventy to 80 percent say ''no increase without any spending reform,'' and yet, all we heard was, ''I will not negotiate.'' This reminds me about the debate in the Paris Peace Talks back in the Vietnam era, the size of the table and the height of the chairs.

Maybe this morning, when the President meets with the Republican leadership and, also, the Democratic leadership previously, we could get the size of the table. You all can have the high chairs. We will take the low chairs. This is silly.

Senator Schumer said that basically we are walking toward a cliff with a blindfold on. I think we have the blindfold off—no action on entitlement reform, no action on tax policy.

I have been to the dinner, with the help of Senator Isakson, at the White House. It was a privilege. But when we talked about how we achieve the grand bargain on tax reform, the President said he needed $800 billion. Now, that price has been raised by the distinguished Majority Leader to $1 trillion. I do not think you are going to find much support on this side of the aisle for that.

Then, when we talked about reform, he said, ''Why can't we take mortgage interest, charitable giving, retirement, just means-test those?'' and then he gave some specific examples. I tried to put in regulatory reform, and I would put that in on the agenda, if you would agree to it or if the President would agree to it.

We are not going to do that. We are not going to means-test everything in the tax code, and we are not going to raise taxes $800 billion or $1 trillion. That is a nonstarter. So I hope that we could do that.

Have you been briefed, or what is the up-to-date news that you can give us about the agenda of this meeting as to the time amount and as to what could be on the table?

Secretary LEW. Senator, the President has been very clear. Congress needs to open the government. Congress needs to make it possible for us to pay our bills, and then he is open to talking about anything. And it not a question of the shape of the table or the size of the table. It is a question of whether there is give and take.

Senator ROBERTS. So you indicate that the President is willing to negotiate, but he is not willing to tell us what agenda or what specific parts of the agenda he might be interested in or not or the time frame?

Secretary LEW. Senator, he has made clear Congress has to open the government, Congress has to make it possible for us to pay our bills, and he is happy to talk about anything. He has made it clear what he would like to get done. We have made it clear in our budget. We have made it clear in numerous communications.

Give-and-take means everyone coming in and doing hard things. He demonstrated his willingness to do hard things. If others are willing to do hard things, maybe we can do something important.

Senator ROBERTS. All right. I am over 13 seconds. I apologize, Mr. Chairman.

I think what you are saying is that, if the government shutdown can be discontinued—everybody wants that, nobody wants a government shutdown, and I do not want to get into that debate again—he is willing to negotiate, but only if we end the shutdown and agree to an extension on the debt limit. Then he may negotiate with an agenda that is just sort of amorphous.

Secretary LEW. He has always been willing to negotiate, just not with the threat of destroying our economy.

The CHAIRMAN. Senator Menendez?

Senator MENENDEZ. Thank you, Mr. Chairman.

Thank you, Mr. Secretary.

My colleagues have already expressed a series of dimensions in which both the shutdown and the threat of default, I think, affect our country domestically economically.

I want to look at a different dimension that both has domestic and global issues. In the other role I play as chairman of the Senate Foreign Relations Committee, I worry about the incredibly, extremely negative effects that the government shutdown and the threat of default have on our foreign policy and our national security, both now and in years to come.

The shutdown and the potential default affected some of America's near-term foreign policy priorities, such as the President not being able to go to the Asian Economic Summit. And his absence, although certainly appropriate due to the crisis, feeds into existing fears, having traveled to the region, that our rebalance to Asia is more rhetoric than reality. And who showed up and was more than willing to fill the void? China. And in doing so, America's loss is China's gain.

This is an opportunity for opening markets for U.S. businesses to sell products and services. This is an opportunity to promote economic and security questions. And I think our allies are going to wonder, is the United States capable of meeting its promises, whether about economic initiatives or security initiatives?

Perhaps the most damaging, I think, and difficult thing to reverse is the impact this has on America's reputation in the world and the economic consequences that flow from that. The entire global financial system depends, in large measure, on the faith that the U.S. Government can and always will pay its debt. And America enjoys the unique privilege of having its currency act as the world's reserve currency.

So it seems to me that, by playing political games, we give credence to other emerging powers, like China and Brazil, who want the world to become less reliant on the dollar, and there are consequences to becoming less reliant on the dollar. Not only does it undermine our standing in the global economic system, it puts our dependability in question with allies.

I know in your role as Treasury Secretary, you fill various international roles within that context. Could you give the committee a sense of the consequences? We have talked about those consequences at home, but there are consequences abroad that affect us here at home.

Secretary LEW. Senator, I think it would be impossible to overstate the importance of the U.S. playing the role in the world that we do in terms of the stability we provide. There is a reason why the dollar is the world's reserve currency.

The world actually counts on us being responsible and making the kinds of decisions that allow them to continue to look to Washington for that kind of stability. We have finance ministers from around the world gathering in Washington this week, and yesterday I met with finance ministers from Africa and finance ministers from Latin America. And it is challenging when they look at you and they ask, ''What is going on in Washington?'' It makes them nervous about their economies, and we need them to have growing demand, because that is good for our economy.

And this question of world reserve currency—it is no secret that there are discussions around the world where others would like there to be a basket of currency that might be used as an alternative to the dollar.

So I have to ask the question. When our role in the world is so important to the United States' well-being, both in terms of security and economic well-being, and to the stability in the world, why would this kind of a manufactured crisis be seen as something that is necessary to pursue, when it undermines that?

So I think the questions you are asking are quite significant.

Senator MENENDEZ. Let me ask you. There are those who suggest, oh, that is not a real issue, because the rest of the world has no place to go.

Secretary LEW. I am not going to speculate on whether someone else will emerge as an alternative, but we are in a place right now where it is important for the United States and the world for us to maintain our position, and we have the capacity to do that. We have the economic ability to do that. It is only a matter of political will.

Senator MENENDEZ. And there is no reason to risk that possibility of finding out whether or not there is some other universe of currencies which people could look to. And there is no reason to risk having the potential economic impacts we can have globally rather than providing domestic opportunities for growth in jobs and opportunities.

Secretary LEW. I certainly think there is no reason. I would go a little further and say that it is against our interest to invite that kind of discussion.

Senator MENENDEZ. Thank you, Mr. Chairman.

The CHAIRMAN. Senator Enzi?

Senator ENZI. Thank you, Mr. Chairman.

Mr. Secretary, I think this is the 11th time I have been through this discussion about "the sky is falling."

Wyoming families are not buying these arguments. They are saying you cannot spend more than you take in, and you definitely cannot keep doing it forever.

I know a person who interned for me several years ago who now is the owner of a major company in Wyoming that operates in four States. And he pays his people well, but every once in a while somebody comes in and says, "I need a pay raise." And he hands them a copy of Dave Ramsey's book and says, "You don't have a problem with income. You've got a problem with spending."

That is what the Wyoming people think. We have a problem with spending, not revenue. They are not interested in having their taxes raised so that we can put more people in the wagon.

I used an example on the Senate floor the other day about how the people working in the private sector get a little upset because government keeps growing, and when it grows, that means there are more people in the wagon and less people pulling the wagon, and they are getting tired of it.

In fact, it is getting pretty hard to pull, and we are not doing anything about it. That is their impression. Why should the goverment be able to increase its revenue? How do we solve this spending problem?

We keep asking for this debt limit increase, and it is always asked for as though, sometime down the road, we are going to negotiate and figure out a way to solve the problem. You mentioned that you would rather we did not have these manufactured crises. America would prefer we do not have these manufactured crises.

I think this is a manufactured crisis, again, because we did not work on it yesterday. The government shutdown—it shows we have not done the budget the way we are supposed to. We are supposed to begin work on the spending bills on April 15th, do one a week, and not get to this continuing resolution situation on October 1st, so everybody will know exactly how much they can spend.

I was invited to Blair House when we were doing Obamacare, and I spent a day of the President chopping down every suggestion that Republicans made. It was a waste of a day. So, when we hear this thing about a willingness to negotiate and, if you have any ideas, get them to me, it is wearing just about as thin as ''the sky is falling.''

So why do you and the President feel we should not be discussing right now this dire financial situation and coming up with a solution that will put a little bit of room in there for something to be done right now?

If people are running up their credit card debt and they need to raise their limit, they are expected to say what they will do in order to be able to take care of their debt, although the credit agencies are not really interested, because the interest rate goes up, which is the same thing we are facing here. You have already said that it has tripled in the last week. So we are running into that same problem.

Why should we not present some kind of a solution? It could be a long-term solution. It does not have to be just a 1-week solution. But we are not even providing a long-term solution. I put out a penny plan that would take care of the deficit in 2 years and result in a balanced budget. Some variation on that might be helpful.

But why do you think the President should not discuss this right now and come up with solutions right now in conjunction with the extension of the debt limit?

Secretary LEW. Senator, those Wyoming families know that, after they have run up their credit card, they do not get to ignore it. They have to pay the bill. The debt limit is just paying our bills. You and I have talked. You know that I would very much like to be in a conversation about long-term, sensible entitlement and tax reform to give the kind of stability going forward that this country needs.

That cannot be done by saying, we will not pay our bills next week. That is what is wrong with engaging right now. The President wants to negotiate.

Senator ENZI. We keep saying that this terrible thing is going to happen, and that this is just paying our bills. How many times can we say it is just paying our bills? The American public does not get that same option.

Secretary LEW. The time to reduce what we need to borrow is when we make the decisions on what we are spending, not after.

If Congress appropriates money, if Congress puts laws in place where people are entitled to benefits, if Congress commits military resources, once those commitments are made, you cannot tell a contractor who is doing work, ''I am not going to pay you because we changed our mind.''

Senator ENZI. Which takes me back to my comment that we should have been doing the spending bills one at a time——

Secretary LEW. I am not disagreeing with you on that.

Senator ENZI [continuing]. In a piecemeal fashion.

The CHAIRMAN. Senator Enzi's time has expired.

Mr. Secretary, it is getting close to 9:35. There are many Senators here who have questions to ask. Senators have been very good about sticking within the limits.

I am hoping you can stay a little bit longer so we can enable Senators to ask their questions. They will probably shorten their questions so that you can stay.

Secretary LEW. It is going to be very difficult to go more than 5 minutes over.

The CHAIRMAN. Well, let us see what we can do.

Senator Carper?

Senator CARPER. Thanks, Mr. Chairman.

Mr. Secretary, thanks for joining us.

I want to say to my colleagues, I just stepped out of the room for a few minutes. I was watching the hearing on television in an adjoining room, and, I must say, people watching this on TV must be frustrated and disappointed with us.

Some of the finest people who serve in the Senate serve on this committee. That is why I wanted to be on this committee. Thoughtful Democrats, Republicans, people willing to be pragmatic, find the middle, find reasonable, principled compromises.

The problem here is pretty simple. Democrats need to support entitlement reform that saves money, saves these programs for the long haul, and is consistent with our obligation to look out for the least of these. That is what we need to do. Republicans need to embrace tax reform that provides some certainty and predictability for businesses and for investors in this country, but at the same time, generates some revenues.

We go back to those 4 years at the end of the Clinton administration when we had four balanced budgets in a row. Revenues as a percentage of gross domestic product were right around 20 percent all 4 years. Those 4 years, spending as a percentage of gross domestic product was right around 20 percent.

Our deficit is down from—it peaked out about 4 years ago at $1.4 trillion. Last year, the year that just ended about 10 days ago, the deficit was about $700 billion. We cut it in half.

Is that enough? No, it is not enough. We need to do more. But we cannot do more unless we do entitlement reform. Over half our spending is entitlement spending. And we cannot do more unless we generate some revenues.

The problem here is—what was the old line in the Paul Newman movie? "What we have here is a failure to communicate." That is part of our problem. We are really talking past each other.

I talk to people all the time, people who have a lot of money, and I tell them they are going to have to pay some more taxes, and they say, "I don't mind paying more taxes. I don't want you to waste my money." That is what they say. "I don't want you to waste my money."

I do not want to waste their money either. I do not think any of us does. Tom Coburn, who used to serve on this committee, and I have introduced legislation that is called the PRIME Act, P-R-I-M-E, and we go at entitlement programs, not to savage old people or poor people, not to hurt the least of these, but to actually save money and preserve these programs for the long haul.

Every one of you on this committee has gotten a letter from Tom Coburn and me asking you to join us as a cosponsor. I hope you will read the letter. I hope you will join us.

Tom Coburn and I held, along with Carl Levin, a hearing on Monday of this week on Social Security Disability. Nobody wants to harm people who are disabled and unable to work. But in Huntington, WV, my native State, by the way, Huntington, WV, one judge approved 99.7 percent of the people who applied for Social Security Disability—99.7 percent. And that kind of thing is the exception. That is the outlier. But there are people who apply and get approved who, frankly, can work and do not deserve to be on disability.

The idea that we cannot somehow meet our moral imperative and also meet a fiscal imperative, that is a fiction. We can do both. And I would say we would really not just boost our approval rating, but we would really instill a lot of confidence in the American people if we would just stop talking past each other and actually work together.

Mr. Secretary, we are going to meet with the President today—Democrats. I presume the Republicans are also going to meet with him today.

Somehow the President has to make it crystal clear that he is willing to negotiate, and I think he has said it—I have heard him say it—on the entitlement stuff. And the Republicans, they have to indicate a willingness to negotiate on tax reform that generates some revenues.

Then there is a matter of trust here. I do not know how to break through it. I really do not know how to break through it.

Any ideas?

Secretary LEW. I think that the kinds of conversations that he is having are meant to try to rebuild some of the trust, to make it clear that, once we get beyond where we are right now, once Congress reopens the government and takes away the threat of default, he has been and remains open to honorable compromise, which means give-and-take. But it has to be a 2-way street, and that has always been the case with any negotiation.

Senator CARPER. All right. Thanks, Mr. Chairman.

The CHAIRMAN. Thank you, Senator.

Senator Brown?

Senator BROWN. Thank you, Mr. Chairman. I will be brief with my questions.

Mr. Secretary, thank you for joining us.

We have heard a lot from the debt limit deniers about how October 17th is not really the day we default. We hear from the debt limit deniers that they are sure that, even if we get there, nothing will happen, since we can pay China and Wall Street first. But the fact of the matter is that that day, October 17th, as you know well, the day we run out of borrowing capacity, is a Thursday, which happens to be the day that Treasury holds its weekly auction to roll over $100 billion in debt.

Comment for us, if you would, what could happen at that auction if we did not raise the debt limit, what could happen if our borrowing costs—would they substantially increase? What would happen if they did increase on Thursday? What would happen if we were unable to roll over the $100 billion in debt?

Secretary LEW. Senator, I am not going to comment on what markets might do. I think the history is clear that anxiety leading up to 2011 caused a bad market reaction.

We have seen in the last few days unease, certainly, with maturities in the period between October 17th and the period immediately after that. I cannot say what the likelihood is of there being a problem. I can say the consequences of any inability for us to roll over would be quite serious.

In terms of the household budget, it is like, instead of having to pay your monthly payment on a mortgage, having to pay the full mortgage, and that would be a problem.

Senator BROWN. Second question. And I will be brief, Mr. Chairman.

Over the last couple of weeks, I have spent a lot of time just calling people in Ohio—community bankers, business executives, entrepreneurs, people running research institutions, hospital executives, small manufacturers—in regard to their party, and I assume, though I do not know their party in most cases, I assume most of them are Republicans because they are in lines of work that might suggest that. But over and over, they say the same thing. Why is this happening? We cannot risk a default.

They do not understand why the government is shut down. They increasingly understand that it is one faction of one party in one house in one branch of government that has brought much of this to a halt.

The National Association of Manufacturers, a large manufacturing association in the country, wrote on Monday, ''The failure of policymakers to address the debt limit is injecting uncertainty into the U.S. economy, hampering the ability of manufacturers and the broader business community to compete and invest and create new jobs.''

For the last several years, since the Health Care Act, since Dodd-Frank, the criticism I hear more than anything from business in my State is uncertainty, uncertainty. When are the Dodd-Frank rules going to be finished? What is going to happen with the implementation of Obamacare? All of these, the uncertainty, that pall that they claim hangs over our country, our economy—I hear it especially from politicians who are critical of many of these programs.

So my question is, if we agree to a short-term clean debt limit increase, does that provide the certainty that we would need to compete?

Secretary LEW. Senator, I have tried to be clear that I think longer certainty would be very good for the economy, and the shorter the period, the less stability it provides.

When you talk about shifting debates to different time periods, retailers are very worried about what happens in November and December if we are going through what we are going through now.

So I think longer is better, but avoiding a crisis is better than having a crisis. And in no case is the President going to end up in a position where the threat of destroying the American economy is the basis for compromising. He wants that negotiation to be on the basis of the kind of give-and-take that honorable compromises come from.

Senator BROWN. Thank you, Mr. Chairman.

This is the worst uncertainty and the most precarious uncertainty I have ever seen in our economy in my time in public office, and what is tragic about it is how self-inflicted it is.

Thank you, Mr. Chairman.

The CHAIRMAN. Thank you, Senator.

Senator Portman?

Senator PORTMAN. Thank you, Mr. Chairman.

Secretary Lew, you have said again today the President will not negotiate on a debt limit, and the President, as was noted earlier, has asserted that there have not been additional items added to debt limits in the past. And, as you and I have talked about and as you know, when you look back at the last 30 years of the history of debt limits, it is the only thing that has worked.

In fact, every significant deficit reduction package that has passed this Congress in the last 30 years has come in the context of a debt limit. I found one that did not. It was in 2005 for about $40 billion, a relatively small deal.

That is the way it has worked, and it is Gramm-Rudman, it is the 1990 Balanced Budget agreement or the Andrews Air Force Base agreement, it is the 1997 Balanced Budget, it is PAYGO rules that many in this committee on the other side of the aisle talk about favorably, and, of course, it is the most recent Budget Control Act just a couple of years ago, all in the context of the debt limit.

So my view is, it is kind of strange the President would, one, not want to negotiate, but, two, say we have not had this stuff. It is all that has worked to deal with this. And you indicated this earlier—it only makes common sense, because it is a tough vote, as you say. Why? Because our constituents do not get it.

Why would you extend the credit card again, go to the limit again without dealing with the underlying problem? And that is why the polling shows that by over 2–1, the American people say, yes, we should extend the debt limit, but only—only if we deal with the underlying problem. And that is all we are asking for.

I am speaking for myself. I will say we need to avoid a debt limit crisis, but we also need to avoid a debt crisis. So, avoiding a debt limit crisis today and avoiding a debt crisis tomorrow should be our objective.

The President himself said, back in 2006, when the debt was half as big as it is today, $8 trillion, and this was a floor speech: "America has a debt problem and a failure of leadership." He said, "I am, therefore, going to oppose the increase in the debt limit." He opposed it when it was half as big as it is today. He said we needed to deal with the underlying problem.

In response to Senator Hatch's question earlier about why the President refuses to deal with the underlying problem—which we all know is the two-thirds of the spending and the biggest part of the spending and the fastest growing part of the spending that is on autopilot, that we do not appropriate every year, which is the mandatory side—in response to that question, you said, and I quote: "He put in his budget significant entitlement spending reforms. He wants to do this.'' And, in fact, you are right. The President's proposal includes a pretty long list of entitlement savings, mandatory savings. It adds up to about $730 billion over 10 years, a step in the right direction.

During that time, by the way, we are likely to add another $8 trillion to the debt, according to CBO, the Congressional Budget Office. But he has $730 billion over 10 years.

Now, not all of those choices reflect my top priorities or others' on this committee, probably, but in a negotiation, you do not get everything you want.

So my question to you today is really very simple. By adding some of those proposals, maybe not all $730 billion, maybe it is $500 billion, maybe it is $400 billion. But by adding some of the President's own proposals to an extension of the debt limit, consistent with what has been done historically and consistent with what the American people are asking for, could we not move forward, and is that not what we ought to be doing, dealing, yes, with the debt limit but also with the underlying problem, and taking the President's own proposals to do it?

Secretary LEW. Senator, on the history of the debt limit, you and I have been back and forth many times. I think it makes a big difference if you tack a debt limit increase onto something that has already been agreed to.

In 1997, the Balanced Budget agreement was all signed and sealed, and then a debt limit increase was put into it. It did not drive it. Nobody threatened default. So I think we are in a different situation since 2011, and that has changed the world.

Senator PORTMAN. Well, nobody has been in default because you have not had a President saying he would not negotiate.

Secretary LEW. And the President has said, and he just repeated this week, he wants to and is prepared to negotiate. I think it is important not to just go through a President's budget and cherry-pick the things that are hard for him to do, you have to look at the things that are hard for others to do, because the negotiation is give-and-take.

If everything is on the table, if we are looking at entitlement reform and tax reform in a way that we join together to solve the problem, there could be a serious conversation.

But I would caution to not take just one side of the ledger.

Senator PORTMAN. Let me focus on that, because the President also said in that budget that he believes we ought to have tax reform. And specifically with regard to corporate tax reform, for the first time in your budget, you indicate it should be revenue-neutral, and I applaud you for that, as you know.

I think that is important. I think it is an urgency right now. If we do not deal with it, we are going to continue to lose more jobs in this country.

My question to you would be, on the President's own proposals on entitlements, I agree there should be a give-and-take, but I am going to say, let us look at the President's own proposals, put those into this debt limit increase, plus directions to the Congress on tax reform, as you all have suggested. Would you all be willing to move that forward?

Secretary LEW. Well, just to be clear, the President's view on the debt limit, he has stated this as clearly as he can: he is not negotiating over the debt limit. The debt limit—Congress has to make it possible to pay our bills. He looks forward to negotiating.

The CHAIRMAN. Senator Bennet, you are next. Senator Bennet?

Secretary LEW. Senator, I hate to call attention to the time, but I am going to be late for another commitment if I——

The CHAIRMAN. Could we have just one more? How about two more?

Secretary LEW. I think if we do two more——

Senator HATCH. This is important.

Secretary LEW. This is very important, Senator.

Senator HATCH. There is nothing more important than this, and I want to make sure everybody on our side at least has a chance.

Senator BENNET. Thank you, Mr. Chairman.

Thank you, Mr. Secretary, for your indulgence. I will just take a few minutes.

In your view, would failing to raise the debt ceiling make our debt limit situation better or worse?

Secretary LEW. Well, it does not do anything good. If the cost of borrowing goes up, it raises our expenditures. It does not reduce them.

Senator BENNET. And if the cost of borrowing went up, just 1 percent or 2 percent—we are at historically low interest rates—what would that cost us?

Secretary LEW. I would have to go back and do the numbers exactly to give you an answer, but these are—we are talking billions of dollars. We are not talking about small numbers.

Senator BENNET. No. I think it is very clear, and Ronald Reagan shared this view—you quoted him earlier—that this would just make matters worse.

Secretary LEW. Unless we were to do something unthinkable and say, we will never pay those bills, you have to pay the bills and you are going to be borrowing money at a higher interest rate. So it only costs——

Senator BENNET. Which means that our interest costs are just going to continue to go up, and our ability to do things like respond to the floods in Colorado or be able to educate our kids will be diminished.

I am going to let you go, because I know you have to go, but I have heard a lot of people on both sides of the aisle today talk about their willingness and their desire to try to meet in the middle, and I think that is important. And I think we need to do that, because I can tell you this: people in Colorado, they are sick and tired of a lot of things about Washington, but what they are mostly sick and tired of is our managing by crisis and, therefore, our inability to manage the affairs of this country in a way, in this case, that does not threaten the full faith and credit of the United States and our ability to have the reserve currency for the world be the American dollar.

Thank you, Mr. Secretary.

The CHAIRMAN. Thank you, Senator.

Senator Toomey?

Senator TOOMEY. Thank you, Mr. Chairman.

Secretary Lew, you have said a couple of times, in reference to previous discussions over the debt limit, that it is different now.

It is true, it is different now. I would argue now it is much more urgent that we deal with the underlying fiscal problem. Now, unlike in past years, we are spending $3.6 trillion. We have run up a string of unprecedented deficits. The modest improvement you alluded to, you know that is temporary, and it is scheduled, if there are no structural changes, for those deficits to get much worse, not terribly far from today.

We now have a total debt that is over 100 percent of our total economic output, I believe, already limiting economic growth and prosperity. We have trillions of dollars of guarantees that we did not use to have. We have tens of trillions of dollars in unfunded liabilities. We have large entitlement programs, the largest of which are all growing faster than our economy and, therefore, are on a completely unsustainable path.

So what is different, it seems to me, is that our situation is much more dire now than it was in previous discussions. Nevertheless, the President is saying, "You give me everything I want, and then we could have a conversation about these things that are important to you."

I still find that shocking. But here is the bottom line, it seems to me. If the President refuses to agree to include even a modest reform that begins to take us in the direction of a more sustainable path in the context of a debt ceiling increase, there appears to be a real chance that this Congress will not pass a debt ceiling increase before October 17th.

Now, I hope that we do pass a debt ceiling increase with appropriate reforms, because there is no question, in my mind, at some point, if we do not raise the debt ceiling, it will become disruptive.

As you know, ongoing tax revenue is only about 85 percent of all the money this government intends to spend in the coming fiscal year. So, if we only get 85 percent of everything we intend to spend in tax revenue, the 15 percent shortfall would have to be covered by borrowing, or else we would not be able to pay everything in full and on time, and that would be disruptive.

But the greatest disruption, by far, would occur if you were to choose to not pay interest on our debt. Senator Cantwell made a very compelling argument about the unique role that U.S. Treasury securities play in the world and for the United States.

So my question for you, Mr. Secretary: as the Secretary of the Treasury, are you prepared to assure us, but, more importantly, the millions of Americans who are investors in U.S. Treasury securities and the entire American economy, that under no circumstances will you permit a missed payment on a U.S. Treasury security obligation?

Secretary LEW. Senator, the only way to make sure we could pay all of our obligations is for Congress to act and raise the debt limit. No President has ever had to decide whether to pay some bills and not others.

Senator TOOMEY. I understand. That is a different question, though.

Secretary LEW. The law is complicated, and I am not the one who makes that decision, as you know. I think that if you look——

Senator TOOMEY. You would make the decision.

Secretary LEW. No, no. It is actually not my decision. It is something that the President would have to decide. And I am telling you that it would put us into default if we went to a place where we could pay one bill and not others.

What would you say to people on Social Security who are not getting paid?

Senator TOOMEY. Mr. Secretary, I have acknowledged that it is very disruptive and that is not where I hope to go, but I only control one vote in the Senate and the administration controls zero, and they control zero votes in the House. So it would seem to me the only appropriate thing to do is plan for a contingency.

So are you telling me that the President would decide to ensure that we would not miss a payment on Treasury securities?

Secretary LEW. Senator, what I am telling you is there is no good solution if Congress fails to raise the debt limit, and that is why the President has called on Congress to raise the debt limit.

You used the number 80–85 percent coverage in terms of revenue. That is an annual average.

Senator TOOMEY. I understand. It is unequal.

Secretary LEW. Some months it is 50 percent.

Senator TOOMEY. That is right. It varies.

Secretary LEW. So the amount that we fall——

Senator TOOMEY. Sometimes it is over 100. I know it.

Secretary LEW [continuing]. Behind in payments is unthinkable. Congress has to do its job and act.

Senator TOOMEY. And I certainly hope that the President will work with us so that we can avoid this, but, frankly, I am shocked that the Secretary of the Treasury will not assure the financial markets, American investors and savers, and the millions of people who hold Treasuries, that they do not have to worry about the security of their Treasuries. I am extremely disappointed.

Secretary LEW. I would refer you back to statements by President Reagan and Secretary Jim Baker, who made the same warnings that I am making, because only Congress can act to raise the debt limit. No President has ever been put in the position of having to figure out what bad option they choose if Congress does not act.

Senator TOOMEY. I understand. I am almost out of time. On Tuesday, the President said, and I quote, ''We plan for every contingency. So, obviously, you know, worst case scenario, there are things we will try to do,'' end quote.

Could you tell us about these contingencies?

Secretary LEW. Senator, the options are all bad.

Senator TOOMEY. I agree.

Secretary LEW. I tried to, earlier, describe how complicated the Federal payment system is. There is no way to make our Federal payment system work well to pick and choose what we pay.

So we are going to be in a place which is uncharted territory, and anyone who thinks it works smoothly—it would not work smoothly.

Senator TOOMEY. Nobody said this would be smooth.

Secretary LEW. It would not work smoothly. It would be chaos.

Senator TOOMEY. The question is whether the Treasury is prepared to try to minimize the disruption.

Secretary LEW. Obviously, we have looked at many options. There have been reports indicating things that have been looked at over the years. Nobody has ever had to put any of these into effect. They are not tested. We have never stopped——

The CHAIRMAN. The Senator's time has expired.

I might say the Secretary has been very patient. I also note there are four Senators left who want to ask questions.

If I might ask, Mr. Secretary, if they can state their questions in 10 seconds each, and you do not have to respond to them——

Secretary LEW. I am happy to do that.

The CHAIRMAN. Ten seconds each and next—just for questioning, because we do not have time—would be Senator Casey.

Senator CASEY. Mr. Secretary, thank you very much for your testimony.

My question relates to Social Security and Medicare and veterans' benefits. I am just going to read two lines from a letter that I got from a constituent talking about her parents.

She said, "At 85 and 83, they should not have this uncertainty," the uncertainty about the impasse. "These should be their golden years. It breaks my heart to see my mother saying she cannot sleep and has a stomach ache from the worry about where our country is headed."

Tell us about the impact of a default when it comes to Social Security, Medicare, and veterans' benefits.

The CHAIRMAN. Senator, I told the Secretary he did not have to answer questions, because so many Senators have to ask. So I appreciate it.

Secretary LEW. I am happy to follow-up.

The CHAIRMAN. Next, Senator Stabenow.

Senator STABENOW. Thank you, Mr. Chairman and Mr. Secretary.

I would just like to ask that we put in the record the complete letter from the National Association of Manufacturers, and I would read one sentence. "A default would put upward pressure on interest rates, raising both short- and long-term cost of capital and discouraging business investment and job creation" in America.

[The letter appears in the appendix on p. 69.]

The CHAIRMAN. Thank you, Senator.

Senator Nelson?

Senator NELSON. Ten seconds.

The CHAIRMAN. Or thereabouts.

Senator NELSON. Mr. Secretary, I am concerned that you have indicated that we might agree to a short-term extension on the debt ceiling, and I think that would be counterproductive. We would be back in this soup right at the end of that short-term extension.

I commend the President for standing firm. We cannot negotiate over the debt ceiling. National security is another consideration. I will put that in the record.

Thank you, Mr. Chairman.

The CHAIRMAN. Thank you, Senator.

Senator Cardin?

Senator CARDIN. Mr. Chairman, thank you.

Secretary Lew, thank you for being here, and thank you for giving us—it is our responsibility to pass the extension of the debt limit. It is Congress's responsibility to do this.

Uncertainty is really hurting this country, and we cannot govern from crisis to crisis. So I strongly support your view that the longer term is what we need here.

My question would be, what legal authority do you have to pick and choose? It seems to me that any analogy we use to a company or a business that cannot pay its bills—there is a limit as to the discretion you have to make those judgments.

I would be interested as to the legal authority you have on prioritization.

The CHAIRMAN. Thank you, Senator.

Other Senators are not here. Obviously, they will want to submit questions to the Secretary.

Secretary LEW. I would be happy to respond.

The CHAIRMAN. Mr. Secretary, you have been very generous with your time. We deeply appreciate it. Thank you very much.

Secretary LEW. Thank you, Mr. Chairman.

The CHAIRMAN. The hearing is adjourned.

[Whereupon, at 9:49 a.m., the hearing was concluded.]

APPENDIX

ADDITIONAL MATERIAL SUBMITTED FOR THE RECORD

Statement of Senator Max Baucus (D-Mont.) on the Need to Avoid Default and Pay America's Bills
As prepared for delivery

On January 27, 1838, a young state legislator named Abraham Lincoln spoke before a gathering in Springfield, Illinois. At the time, America was a deeply-divided nation and Lincoln warned that the greatest threats to the democracy were internal.

He said, "If [danger] ever reaches us, it must spring up amongst us; it cannot come from abroad. If destruction be our lot, we must ourselves be its author and finisher. As a nation of freemen we must live through all time or die by suicide."

The actions of the past few weeks — the extremism of a small group of members in the House of Representatives — have crippled Congress and put our nation on a very perilous path.

For more than 200 years, the United States has been true to its word, honored its obligations and paid its debts. Yet today, a small group of hardliners is using our economy as a bargaining chip to repeal the Affordable Care Act.

Let me be very clear: We're not going to let that happen. The Affordable Care Act is the law of the land. It is not going to be dismantled in this budget fight. This issue is not up for debate.

I am always open to this committee working together to strengthen the law to better serve the American people. But as the President said, we cannot negotiate under the threat of default on the nation's bills.

Before any debate, before any deliberation, we need to reopen the government and pay the nation's bills – no strings attached.

Then, we need to return to regular order around here. Working together, we must address the nation's long-term budget challenges, including entitlement and tax reform.

But right now, we need to prevent another self-inflicted wound to America's economy. That is what defaulting on the debt is: a self-inflicted wound with global consequences.

The deadline is fast approaching. In seven days, the United States Treasury will have exhausted all "extraordinary measures" to stay under the debt limit. In seven days, the United States will be at risk of defaulting on payments. The United States of America — the richest, most powerful nation in the world — will be forced to look for loose change in the sofa in order to pay its bills.

While the government shutdown has been disruptive, a default would be a financial heart attack. It would have widespread, long-term economic consequences. Financial markets are already showing serious signs of stress. The Dow has dropped more than 800 points over the last three weeks. And the one-month Treasury bill rate has risen to its highest level since the 2008 fiscal crisis.

If the debt ceiling is breached, the government would immediately have to slash federal spending by 20 to 30 percent, driving the nation back into a recession.

The pain would be felt across every sector of society. Social Security and Medicare would be cut, veterans' benefits would be slashed, funding for highways would be hit– every government program would be devastated by deep cuts.

Families would feel it firsthand with dramatic drops in their retirement savings. Jobs would be lost. Home values would plunge. Interest rates on mortgages and student loans would soar.

Some have said we can avoid default by prioritizing U.S. payments — paying bondholders and interest on the debt. But they fail to mention this scheme would force Treasury to pick which programs to pay, forcing vital programs like Social Security and Medicare to compete for funding. The idea is just irrational.

A default would have a catastrophic impact on the global economy as well. Jim Yong Kim, the president of the World Bank warned a default could have dire consequences for the world's economy. Christine Lagarde, the managing director of the International Monetary Fund, said it is "mission-critical" that the debt limit be resolved as soon as possible.

This is serious. The whole world is watching. Our actions here in the next couple of days will have global implications. We are the most important economy in world. The dollar is the world's reserve currency. Our Treasury bonds are the backbone of the international financial system. A default could put the global economy in chaos.

Last week, Treasury warned us that a default could cause a "financial crisis and recession that could echo the events of 2008 or worse."

Have people here forgotten what happened in 2008? The collapse of Lehman Brothers set off a financial earthquake. Markets plunged, unemployment surged and America's confidence was shattered to the core. The 2008 crisis upended lives across the country. The aftermath of which can still be felt to this day.

We cannot let that happen again. We have a responsibility to avoid another economic disaster.

Our leadership — our resolve — will be tested in the coming days. We — all of us here in this room —have an opportunity to pull America back from the brink.

Earlier this week, I introduced a bill with Leader Reid that would get us past this stalemate. The bill extends the nation's borrowing authority through the end of 2014, past the midterm elections. It is a clean increase without any amendments. It simply allows the United States to pay its debts and avoid a catastrophic default.

This is only a short-term solution, but it will help pull us back from the edge. It will allow us all here to pause, take a deep breath and once again try and come together to move forward.

I have been here in the Senate for close to 35 years — in Congress going on 39. I've seen my fair share of partisan fights. Never in my time here have I seen Washington so angry, so gridlocked or so broken. It doesn't have to be that way.

I know the public might find it hard to believe, but there are some reasonable people here in Congress. There are many who want to do what is right. There are many who want to work together to conduct the business of our nation.

I would say to them — and to all my colleagues — now is the time. Now is the time for Congress to stop refighting old battles. Now is the time for Congress to come together and do what is right for our nation. Now is the time for Congress to come together and reopen the government and fulfill America's financial obligations.

I began my remarks with a quote from President Lincoln and thought it appropriate to conclude with one as well. Lincoln once said, "I am a firm believer in the people. If given the truth, they can be depended upon to meet any national crises."

That is why we are here today. We need to give the American people the truth — the real facts. Only then, when everyone understands the real risks at hand, will we be able to meet this national crisis.

###

STATEMENT OF HON. ORRIN G. HATCH, RANKING MEMBER
U.S. SENATE COMMITTEE ON FINANCE HEARING OF OCTOBER 10, 2013
THE DEBT LIMIT

WASHINGTON – U.S. Senator Orrin Hatch (R-Utah), Ranking Member of the Senate Finance Committee, delivered the following opening statement at a committee hearing examining the nation's debt limit with Treasury Secretary Jack Lew:

Mr. Chairman, I want to thank you for holding today's hearing on the debt limit. I also want to welcome Secretary Lew to this hearing today.

During debate over a debt limit increase in 2006, then-Senator Obama stated that: "The fact that we are here today to debate raising America's debt limit is a sign of leadership failure."

Leadership, he said: "means that the buck stops here. Instead, Washington is shifting the burden of bad choices today onto the backs of our children and grandchildren. America has a debt problem and a failure of leadership. Americans deserve better."

Secretary Lew, on the day then-Senator Obama spoke about our debt problem, our gross debt was $8.3 trillion. It is now more than twice that, currently standing at $16.7 trillion. That represents 107 percent of the size of our economy. And, as the Congressional Budget Office has made clear, this poses large economic and fiscal risks.

During that same 2006 debt limit debate, then-Senator Biden said: "My vote against the debt limit increase cannot change the fact that we have incurred this debt already, and will no doubt incur more. It is a statement that I refuse to be associated with the policies that brought us to this point."

What a difference in attitude there has been since then.

Now President Obama and Vice President Biden preside over an administration that tells us that raising the debt limit, in your words Secretary Lew, "simply allows us to pay our bills."

Secretary Lew, you have also publicly stated that only Congress has the power to lift the debt limit.

Now, while it is ostensibly true that Congress has the power to raise the debt limit, there will be no increase if the President does not agree.

At the same time, despite your public statements to the contrary, it is not true that raising the limit has only to do with spending Congress already approved. This line of argument is based on a premise that Congress makes spending decisions unilaterally, and that the Executive Branch plays no role in the process.

That premise is simply false.

No amount of spending can be enacted without the President signing it into law.

Furthermore, while President Obama's budgets have not been well received by even the Democrats in Congress, the President has, traditionally, been deeply involved in Congress's efforts to set spending priorities.

The administration also issues Statements of Administration Policy and veto threats on spending bills and other pieces of legislation.

Presidents work with Congress all the time to enact their domestic agendas. We all remember how President Obama unveiled and pushed his trillion dollar stimulus through a Democratic Congress that he then signed into law.

In addition, this President has made unilateral decisions – with no input from Congress – that have had an impact on federal spending. For example, there was the decision to delay the Employer Mandate under Obamacare, which CBO tells us will add an additional $12 billion to our deficit.

Congress never voted on the delay. It was a unilateral choice made through rulemaking at the Treasury Department.

So, in short, the commonly repeated notion that questions surrounding spending and the debt limit are Congress's and Congress's alone to answer is, to put it mildly, a case of false advertising on the part of the Obama Administration.

There have been several other instances of false advertising from the administration concerning the debt limit.

One is the President's claim that non-budget items have never before been attached to the debt limit increase – a claim to which a fact checker at the Washington Post assigned the maximum four Pinocchios.

In fact, of the 53 debt limit increases passed since 1978 – under both Republican and Democratic Presidents – only 26 were "clean."

Another is that, in 2011, we entered some sort of brave new world in which, for the first time in recent history, people were commenting on an inability of Treasury to make timely payment on incoming due obligations.

If you would just go back to President Clinton's administration and read some press conferences held by then-Treasury Secretary Rubin, you will see that this claim is also false.

Mr. Chairman, I ask permission to enter a reprint of a press conference in 1995 with then Treasury Secretary Rubin and then White House Chief of Staff Panetta that supports this position, along with an associated article from the New York Times.

Now, Secretary Lew, I hope that, during today's hearing, we do not simply regress into comparative recollections of history. What is at stake is too big for that.

The issue we face is yet another debt limit increase.

There have been seven debt limit increases since the President came into office, collectively raising the limit from $11.3 trillion to the current $16.7 trillion, a cumulative increase of $5.4 trillion.

When talking about the future increases in the debt limit, all the administration will say is that: 1) they want a "clean" increase, and 2) they refuse to negotiate.

We don't know what they mean by a "clean" increase. We don't even know how much of an increase they want or for how long. Apparently, even making such desires known would constitute a negotiation.

This posture is neither productive nor helpful toward resolving the current impasse over the debt limit.

Essentially, what the administration appears to be saying is that it is ENTIRELY up to Congress to increase the debt limit and to decide how much and for how long.

This, of course, raises more questions than it answers.

For instance, does it mean that, if Congress chooses to enact a two-week clean debt limit increase, the President will sign it?

According to the administration's public statements, because Congress is solely responsible for increasing the debt limit, such a hypothetical stop-gap would be fine if that's what Congress chose to do. Yet, somehow, I don't think that's what the President is looking for when it comes to the debt limit.

In just the past couple of days, the President has expressed willingness to entertain a short-term increase in the limit, which sounds like a willingness to negotiate terms. Sadly, the President's statements are still short on details.

Secretary Lew, the lack of real engagement on the part of the administration is just one of the elements of the current debt limit debate that I find disconcerting.

It is also disconcerting to have administration officials, including you, publicly questioning sentiments of Americans and financial market participants, and suggesting that people may be too calm in an apparent effort to whip up uncertainty in the markets.

It is disconcerting that you have suggested that payments of Social Security benefits to retirees and disabled American workers are at risk, especially since you are a Trustee of the Social Security trust funds.

It is disconcerting that administration officials are sounding alarms of emerging risks to financial stability arising from the debt limit impasse, while, at the same time, the Financial Stability Oversight Council, which you Chair, has been silent and refuses to tell the American people how it would respond to these risks.

Finally, it is disconcerting that the administration refuses, in the context of the debt limit, to even have a conversation with anyone concerning our unsustainable entitlement programs, which everyone agrees are the main drivers of our debt.

The President has, thus far, refused to seriously discuss structural entitlement reforms without assurance that he first gets yet another tax hike. More often than not, what we hear from the administration on entitlements is a series of disclaimers as to what reform proposals they will no longer consider. And, that list seems to get larger every day.

The biggest question I have is: If the Obama Administration won't negotiate on entitlements in the context of the debt limit, when will they negotiate on entitlements?

Secretary Lew, I will remind you that I have put forth five modest reform proposals for our health entitlement spending, and personally gave them to the President earlier this year. You also have copies of these proposals.

Yet, to this day, I have yet to hear a response. I cannot even get mere conversations from the administration about my proposals that I offered in good faith, well before the debt limit was even an issue.

Most recently, the Senate Majority Leader has introduced a "clean" debt limit bill that would increase the limit until January 1, 2015, which will likely raise the limit by $1.3 trillion or more. That, apparently, is the position of the Senate Democratic Leadership, but is somewhat inconsistent with the President's recent willingness to accept a short-term increase in the debt limit.

As you can see, Secretary Lew, we have a lot to discuss today. My hope is that, during the course of this hearing, we can get a real sense of where the administration wants to go with regard to the debt limit.

I also hope that we can get past the arguments that have thus far dominated the administration's rhetoric regarding this issue.

Our nation's debt is now larger as a share of our economy than at any time since World War II.

Despite the rhetoric of the administration, our growing debt is not solely the result of decisions made by Congress.

It is not all due to the financial crisis.

And, it is not all the result of tax relief enacted under the Bush administration.

Instead, it is a problem that all of us – both Congress and the Executive Branch – need to deal with. And, the only way to responsibly deal with it is to confront our unsustainable entitlement spending, which will require the administration to do something it is now refusing to do, which is negotiate.

Secretary Lew, as President Obama said in 2006 regarding the debt limit, Americans deserve better. Thank you, Mr. Chairman.

###

Press Briefing by Chief of Staff Leon Panetta and Treasury Secretary Robert Rubin
November 9, 1995

The Briefing Room

12:20 P.M. EST

SECRETARY RUBIN: Good morning. I don't think it's afternoon yet. Oh, I guess it is afternoon. Okay, we're out of sync. I revise my comment. Good afternoon. Leon Panetta and I will speak a bit about events that are going on with respect to debt limit, continuing resolution-related matters. I'll start with the debt limit.

The President will veto the House debt limit because it moves America closer to default. It is crafted to coerce the President into signing a budget that he has already said he will not sign because he believes it is unsound for the future of this country. The consequences that this legislation is not -- I will repeat -- this legislation is not a debt ceiling increase, it is a shortcut to default on the full faith and credit of the United States of America for the first time in our history.

As written, the legislation cuts off our ability to borrow on December 12th. It then pushes us closer to the brink of default by repealing existing powers the Treasury has with respect to cash management to prevent default. The bill also rolls back the limit on outstanding debt to a level $100 billion below the current debt limit, an action that extraordinary and perhaps unprecedented.

Finally, the bill attempts to design a system of priority of payments to certain federal beneficiaries that would take effect when the debt limit is reached. As a practical matter, it would take several months to put those processes into place. So, during those several months, even those protected beneficiaries would, in fact, not be protected. Moreover, all other federal payments not identified as protected -- for example, Medicare payments and tax refunds -- would be jeopardized under any circumstances.

In summary, this legislation will either force national default or coerce the President into signing a budget that he will not sign as being against the national interest.

Let me conclude if I may with a few additional observations. For over 200 years, America has never defaulted on its debt. Our creditworthiness is an enormously valuable national asset, and it must not be relinquished. Default will call into question the integrity of the United States with respect to meeting our commitments.

When you create a question mark about meeting your commitments in the financial marketplace, that has real and serious consequences. Default would increase the cost of federal borrowing by virtue of having created a question remark with respect to our integrity, with respect to meeting commitments, would increase the cost of borrowing for the federal government for as far into the future as you can see -- 10, 15, 20 years from now we would pay more for money by virtue of having tainted our financial reputation.

Moreover, the effect of default is particularly critical when the nation enters a period of uncertain circumstances, when there are difficult circumstances to deal with and your reputation in the financial marketplace is most important. Default would also affect private sector borrowing costs because much of private sector borrowing is geared to federal interest costs. For example, variable rate mortgages are geared to federal government borrowing costs; so is much corporate debt and much consumer debt.

Finally, the example of the largest nation in the world defaulting on its debt would be an horrendous example in the global financial markets as other nations around the world make the very difficult decisions they have to make when they are in difficult circumstances with respect to meeting their commitments or taking what sometimes seems to be the easier way out and defaulting.

Our reputation with respect to meeting our commitments must never be sacrificed. And that is why default should be taken off the table as a tactic with respect to resolving the budget debate.

Unless the Congress acts to increase the debt limit with a clean debt limit increase bill, and raises the debt ceiling, and does so before November 15th, Treasury will be forced to take extraordinary actions to stave off default. As I have said in many instances before, both to the press and in letters to the leadership, these actions are without precedent; they are costly; they require legal judgments to be made based on the facts then before me as we come up against the brink of default, but they are definitely preferable to default itself.

There is a much better alternative before the Congress. It should pass a clean extension of the government's borrowing authority. The debt limit is not about deficit reduction, it is about meeting past obligations. Progress on balancing the budget, progress that this administration is fully committed to, will occur only by making the difficult decisions about spending cuts, and that must be done in a non-coercive environment and in accordance with usual legislative procedures -- public debate, public debate -- back into Congress and then decisions being made.

Let me conclude by repeating the comment I made earlier because I think it is really key to this entire matter with respect to the House debt ceiling proposal, and that is that this legislation is not a debt ceiling increase; it is a short cut to default on the full faith and credit of the United States of America for the first time in its history.

MR. PANETTA: The debate over how to achieve a balanced budget is, I think, one of the most significant of our lifetimes because it really does involve deep, fundamental issues about not just our values but the future course of this country. We're deciding the future of Medicare and Medicaid. We're deciding whether this nation should maintain its commitment to education, protection of the environment. We're really deciding whether to raise taxes on working families and reduce them on the wealthy, or give middle-class families the kind of tax cut they deserve.

These are large and fundamental issues. And there are legitimate differences between the parties as we approach these issues. They ought to be fully debated. They ought to be fully decided, but not in the context of crisis.

The President has presented a balanced budget. The Republicans have rejected the President's proposal out of hand. And they continue to reject the President's proposal with every amendment and proposal that passes on the House floor which continues to contain the most extreme elements of their budget.

Therefore, the Republicans are now obviously resorting to a form of blackmail in order to push their agenda onto the country. The President has made clear that he will not allow that to happen, that either he or the country should be forced to decide between whether we destroy Medicare or whether we shut down the government. That is not an acceptable choice. That is blackmail.

The President has consistently and repeatedly told the leadership of the Congress that he wants them to pass the legislation with regards to the debt ceiling clean, without any extraneous provisions, without provisions that seek to implement any element of their agenda without provisions that tie the hands of the administration. When it comes to the issue of default, Mr. Secretary has said this ought to be faced directly and cleanly, and it ought not to be part of the larger debate with regards to the budget.

The President has said that consistently. He said it in this room on October 25th, he said it in his radio address on October 28th; he told the bipartisan leadership exactly that in the meeting we had last Thursday on November 1st.

Again, the President cannot, on behalf of the nation, allow the Republicans to basically threaten the country into choosing between whether or not we shut down the government or force a default, or accept the cuts that they've proposed in Medicare and Medicaid and education and the environment and their proposed tax increases on working families. That is just not a choice that this President is going to accept.

Secretary Rubin has been writing and talking to the leadership for months about the issue of default, and he has again repeated those concerns today. Yet they continue to load the bill with regards to the debt ceiling with key elements of their agenda and with straight-jacket provisions that would virtually force the country into a default. They included issues like elimination of the Commerce Department, reg reform, habeas corpus, seven years. There are a number of issues that they're now adding to the debt ceiling, which, again, are totally unacceptable. And the President will veto that proposal if it comes to the White House.

The same is true, I should add, for the continuing resolution to keep government services available to the American people. The continuing resolution expires on Monday night -- this Monday night, at midnight. The bill passed by the House that they approved yesterday -- the continuing resolution that was approved yesterday basically, again, tries to push the same kind of choice on the American people, which is we want to double the premiums on Medicare recipients, slash education, or we will cut off all services to the American people. Again, that is unacceptable.

The continuing resolution that we are currently operating with, that we worked out with the leadership in a cooperative fashion, that was approved by both the House and the Senate and is now in effect is an even-handed measure. Congress should simply extend that measure so that we can continue whatever discussions we should have with regards to the budget.

Let me make clear that the reason that we're at this point is that the Congress again has not finished its work both with regards to the appropriations as well as the budget. Of the 13 appropriations bills, they have only sent two to the President that he has signed. This is the worst record of a Congress since 1987 when it comes to appropriations bills, and they still have not passed any form of balanced budget bill and sent that to the President. They are now 40 days past deadline. Congress should stop, obviously, playing the games that they're currently involved with, get down to business, do their work, send the President a clean debt ceiling bill to avert default, send us a simple extension of the continuing resolution and then let's all get back to work on the broader issues involved in the budget debate.

The concern, obviously, that we have is that what we're facing right now is not exactly a secret, it is, in part a design that the Speaker and the others have spoke to for these last few months that they are essentially trying to threaten the country and threaten the President with the choice between accepting their priorities or facing the prospect of default. So this is basically an implementation of that strategy.

I think what the Republican leaders have to understand and realize is that they are now the majority party and that they, as the majority party, have to accept a degree of responsibility for helping to govern this country and to govern it in a responsible fashion. They cannot act like a minority when they are, in fact, responsible for helping to govern this country. This means that they have to begin acting like adults, live up to their responsibilities, even the unpleasant ones. The debt limit is not an easy vote. I understand that. It's a tough vote. But it's one of the responsibilities of governing. They should do it now before they cause even greater uncertainty in the markets.

The President is looking forward to signing into law before the end of this year legislation that balances the budget. But it has to be legislation that balances the budget without harming our senior citizens, without harming our children, and protecting again our investments in education, in protecting our environment, in providing the kind of targeted tax cut that we think is necessary for middle-class families in this country.

So he will do his part -- he will do his part -- the President of the United States will do his part to ensure that the United States lives up to its obligations and its financial obligations, as well as its governmental obligations to the people of the United States. He fully expects that the Congress will do the same. We hope that the Speaker and the Majority Leader will recognize and implement their responsibility to govern.

Q: Leon, so far we understand that there have been some meetings and you're going to meet again this afternoon about some orderly process of beginning to shut down the government. Can you tell us what that would involve and what services will no longer be provided if the CR is not reauthorized?

MR. PANETTA: Well, we have, beginning in the latter part of the summer, asked all of the departments to prepare plans in the event that we would have to face the situation. It was one that we thought we might have to face on October 1. But because, again, the leadership took the responsible approach, we were able to agree to a continuing resolution that was acceptable to all sides and we avoided that.

Nevertheless, each of the departments and agencies in the federal government have a plan to implement if, in fact, we are ordered to shut down. We expect that the Director of the Office of Management and Budget Alice Rivlin will present a briefing on what specific steps have to be taken on Saturday. I can just tell you, as indicated in The Washington Post this morning, that we're looking at the prospect of 800,000 people having to be furloughed immediately, and there will be additional steps that would have to be taken in order to comply with the law if, in fact, we are forced to shut down the government.

Q: Does this mean that there won't be drug cases being made, that there won't be people getting Social Security checks? I mean, for people who are home wondering, what does it mean for them, can you tell us what that means?

MR. PANETTA: It will clearly have a lot of implications here -- certainly, for the 800,000 who are on furlough, but more importantly, as an example, new claims on Social Security will not be processed, new claims for veterans will not be processed, and there will be other agencies, such as the Environmental Protection Agency that will have to close much of its operation. There are some agencies that are allowed to continue under a Justice Department opinion because of the urgency of the operations that they work with. And as I said, there will be a more definitive presentation of all of that on Saturday. But let's make no mistake about it, when you shut down government services to the people of this country it is going to have an impact on those who, frankly, are innocent victims of this political debate. It just simply should not happen.

Q: Mr. Panetta, if there is no continuing resolution by Monday night's deadline will the President go to Boston as scheduled Monday night and then go to Japan later in the week as scheduled?

MR. PANETTA: All of that, obviously, is -- we're going to continue to review what steps the President has to take in line with what the Congress does. Our hope is that we won't reach that point. Our hope is that, obviously, the leadership will agree to a clean debt ceiling increase and clean extension of the continuing resolution, and that we won't have to in any way bring crisis upon the country. But the President -- all of us are reviewing the situation on Capitol Hill and, obviously, if it gets to that point we'll have to revisit those decisions.

Q: Legally, legally, is there an opinion yet on whether the President can go to Japan if there is shutdown of the federal government?

MR. PANETTA: I believe under the rulings that it is possible for the President to be able to continue to make that kind of trip because it involves foreign policy of the country and our national security. But I also have to say to you that if we --

if, indeed, we are at a point where we have been forced into a default, then that is a decision that we are going to have to look at at that point.

Q: Secretary Rubin, you asked about -- or you said in your remarks Treasury will be forced to take extraordinary actions to stave off default. What do you mean by that?

SECRETARY RUBIN: Well, we have said in letters to the leadership that there are a number of powers that we have -- the very powers that this House legislation is attempting to take or would take away -- that if we can make the judgment at the time we face going over the debt limit or face default can be invoked would enable us to work our way through the default date and particularly with the Civil Service Retirement Act and the G Fund. And they are both -- they both have provisions in them which allow them to be used for debt management purposes. But you have to make a legal judgment at the time that you get up against the debt limit and you get up against default as to whether or not the statute is applicable to the facts at that given moment. And that's the decision that I will have to make at that time.

Q: How much time will that buy you?

Q: Yes. How much time will they buy you? How much money is available to you? And do you have any alternatives besides the retirement fund and the G Fund?

SECRETARY RUBIN: There are other measures we can consider using. They all involve very difficult practical and legal issues. We are working on them. In terms --

Q: Can you tell us what those might be?

Q: How about the Bank Insurance Fund, can you use that?

SECRETARY RUBIN: No, we have no intent of using the Bank Insurance Fund. I don't want to go through all of these items, for various reasons. But let me say that, in facing the question of November 15, the two powers that are at issue were the two that are addressed in the House legislation, Civil Service Retirement Act and the G Fund -- in terms of how long they can take us, that once again becomes a question of how large -- what the inflows and outflows will be. And as we've said all along, in a budget of $1.5 trillion, these numbers, although we make estimates every day, these numbers vary considerably, and as time goes on they may be different than our estimates.

Number two, there are serious legal questions that you have to continue addressing with respect to the applicability of the statutes to the fact at any given moment. So I think that's really a question that, while we have made some very preliminary judgments on, I would not want to answer in a public forum.

Q: But are you talking of days or weeks?

Q: Given the historical and long-lasting impacts you've cited about default and your tremendous concerns -- the letter you've released today -- do you believe that it is more important to resist the Republican budget and go into default? Is the Republican budget worse than the long-term consequences to this country of a default?

SECRETARY RUBIN: I think the two things are undesirable. I think default should be absolutely be off the table. I don't think default should be part of this debate. In any negotiation -- and I've done very large numbers of negotiations in my private sector life before I came here -- there are all sorts of taxes you can consider, but there are some things that you say simply are beyond the acceptable, and default is beyond the acceptable in terms of the national self interest.

In terms of budgets, my view is that the congressional majority's budget, the reconciliation bill they've put forward, is not the proper course for the future of this country. I believe that the President should veto, as he said he will.

Q: But there seems to be a distance between you and the President on this issue. He believes that it's better to go into default than to accept the Republican budget.

SECRETARY RUBIN: No, that's not what he believes at all. He believes that --

Q: That's what he said.

SECRETARY RUBIN: No, it's not what he said. What he said is that default should absolutely be off the table, that we should separate the debt limit from the budget process, get a clean increase in the debt limit, and then go on and resolve this budget debate through a public debate, through congressional process and through interaction between the administration and the Congress.

Q: Mr. Rubin, even though that's a linkage that you don't like, it is linked, and I wonder if you could prioritize. Will you let the government go into default in favor of --

SECRETARY RUBIN: I don't accept the premise of your question. I don't think they're linked at all. I think that the debt limit, as I've said now many times, should be separated from the budget process, the debt limit should be increased.

Actually, what really should happen is, the debt limit should be increased to a period beyond the budget process, and then the budget process should be resolved through the usual legislative processes, including public debate. What is actually happening -- another way to look at this whole thing is that what is really happening is that there is an effort to coerce the President into doing something that he feels is very much against the interests of the nation, and that really is an effort to undermine the normal legislative processes that go on in this country.

MR. PANETTA: Let me just speak to that. This is not a real choice. This is a false choice. If the Republicans really believe in the validity of their budget let them take it to the American people. Let them get the support of the American people on their issues. Let them debate it openly. Let them go through the process the way every other party has had to go through a process when you want to get something done. But don't, don't, put a gun to the head of the President and head of the country and say, you don't accept our priorities, you don't accept what we want to do to Medicare and Medicaid or what we want to do to education -- we're going to blow you apart. That's a form of terrorism. We are not going to accept that.

Q: There is an opinion in the bond market that it's possible to take a hit in terms of a default, knowing that it's a price to be paid for long-term deficit reduction. In other words, that the risk is worth facing and even confronting. Default is worth it -- that's the argument that is made by some in the market. What do you say to that?

SECRETARY RUBIN: I say it's a false choice. I think what the President has said is exactly right -- we need to take the debt ceiling, get it out beyond the budget process, and then continue the deficit reduction process he began in 1993. Through the budget process he's brought the deficit down to half -- roughly half of what it was when he took office. We can continue that process, put his budget in place, and we can go to balance. My answer is the false choice.

Q: Mr. Panetta, excuse me for changing the subject, but I wondered if you'd spoken with Hazel O'Leary about the article in the Wall Street Journal today and what your reaction was to that report?

MR. PANETTA: Well, I was very concerned with the article that appeared in the Wall Street Journal and called the Secretary and asked for a full report on what was behind this particular situation. And I want to give her the opportunity to present me with that report before making any further decisions.

Q: So when will she do that?

Q: When do you get the report?

MR. PANETTA: I've asked for that, hopefully, by the end of the day.

Q: Mr. Panetta, is this the kind of situation that might require a resignation?

MR. PANETTA: I don't want to speculate on that. I want to see what the report is first.

Q: Mr. Panetta, accepting your qualms about the debt ceiling, with respect to the continuing resolution, you're an old budget tactician from Congress, why shouldn't they load it up with all the -- I mean, I understand that you don't like it, but why shouldn't they load it up with all the things they want to try to force your hand? Isn't that part of the normal legislative process and tactics, if you leave default aside?

MR. PANETTA: Well, look, again, I've always assumed that there would be a point at which, frankly, there would be a discussion as to what we ought to do with regards to the CR. When we did the continuing resolution last time I had the opportunity to sit down with Congressman Livingston, Senator Hatfield, and I think we were able in a rational way to try to work out some give-and-take that resulted in a final continuing resolution. That's the best way to make it happen.

The problem is that once you engage in the process of loading up a bill with objectionable items, then you basically are in a fight in which both sides dig in. And suddenly, what happens is, once a member has been forced to vote on a continuing resolution that contains some of these extreme elements, that member is stuck. And rather than get to the situation where you're putting people in that kind of lock, why not try to -- and this is essentially what I argued with the leadership last Thursday -- let's understand where we are. The President is not going to accept your budget at this point. Let's provide a clean extension of the debt ceiling. Let's provide a clean extension of a CR, send us your bill; the President will veto it; then hopefully we can engage in discussions that can bring us an agreement on a balanced budget. Now, that's where we are, and it seems to me that's the responsible way to try to proceed here.

But what you're seeing happening right now is, very frankly, a path that clearly is going to lead to a veto if they proceed the way they are. We ought to be talking; we ought to be discussing the approach there. I had asked both the Speaker and the Majority Leader Dole on the airplane, please do not proceed with a continuing resolution or a debt ceiling proposal until you've talked with us about it in order to try to avoid this problem. That has not happened.

Q: Mr. Panetta, is there a change in the President's earlier support for the Senate version of welfare reform?

MR. PANETTA: I think what you'll see -- and Alice Rivlin will be briefing on the report that's coming out with regards to the impact of the various welfare reform proposals, as well as the budgets that are up there -- it basically reflects what the President stated -- has stated in his radio address and has continued to state, which is that the Senate version on welfare reform is a good beginning and a step in the right direction, but there are improvements that have to be made in the conference.

We have made clear that there are improvements that have to be made, particularly with regards to children and particularly with regards to trying to protect states that have to deal with these issues in terms of work and responsibility. So what I think this report helps us do, very frankly, is it gives us some momentum to urge the conferees to try to implement the improvements that we've requested.

We have not changed our position, if that's what you're asking.

Q: Precisely, what does the President want changed in the bill, or added to the bill, or whatever, before he would sign it?

MR. PANETTA: It's going to be laid out specifically in the report. It was laid out in the letter that Alice Rivlin sent to the Congress. We specifically are asking for improvements with regards to the immigration issue; we're asking for additional funding with regards to the contingency funds; we're asking for additional funds with regards to child care and child support; we're asking for revisions on the SSI provisions and on the food stamp provisions. Those are the key elements. The rest of it will be presented to you in the report.

Q: Secretary Rubin, can you stave off default with the Civil Service Retirement and the G-7 -- can you stave that off for a matter of days, a matter of weeks, hours?

SECRETARY RUBIN: I believe that with the powers that I now have as Secretary of the Treasury, assuming that I make the requisite legal judgments when we come up against the debt limit and the day to default, that we can work our way through this for some period of time. And I think I'd rather not be more precise than that other than to say for some period of time.

But meanwhile, what should happen is that Congress should fulfill its responsibility and act a clean debt ceiling increase and get this out of the budget process so that we can then go on and resolve the budget debate.

Q: Secretary Rubin, do you see any signs that foreign investors are beginning to lose faith or get nervous about holding U.S. bonds or the dollar?

SECRETARY RUBIN: I think, rather than comment on investors' reactions at the moment, which I have resisted doing with respect to all markets since I've been Secretary of the Treasury, I would rather go back to the comments I made before, that as a matter of policy -- of policy -- undermining the integrity of the United States with respect to meeting its commitments should be absolutely off the table for all concerned and these processes go forward.

This is very, very serious business and it's going to affect the future of this nation for a long, long time to come.

THE PRESS: Thank you.

END 12:51 P.M. EST

Citation: William J. Clinton: "Press Briefing by Chief of Staff Leon Panetta and Treasury Secretary Robert Rubin", November 9, 1995. Online by Gerhard Peters and John T. Woolley, *The American Presidency Project*. http://www.presidency.ucsb.edu/ws/?pid=59671.

House and Senate Act to Avert a Default

By DAVID E. ROSENBAUM
Published: November 10, 1995

With the Government only a few days away from a theoretical financial breakdown, Republicans in Congress and Democrats in the White House fired volleys of charges and countercharges at one another today but moved not an inch toward resolving their differences.

At nightfall, the House of Representatives approved a bill that would extend the Government's authority to borrow money until mid-December. But the measure was cast in such a way that it cannot pass the Senate, much less be signed by the President.

A couple of hours later, the Senate voted 50 to 46, mostly along party lines, to approve a bill that would give departments and agencies money to spend through Dec. 1. The bill must go back to the House because it differs from a companion measure passed Wednesday night by the House in the way it treats lobbying by organizations that receive grants from the Federal Government.

Later in the evening, the Senate approved legislation to extend the Government's authority to borrow money, voting 49 to 47 to raise the debt ceiling.

At the White House, President Clinton was standing by, his veto pen at the ready, waiting to see exactly what, if anything, the Republican Congress would agree on.

The day began with the observation by Michael D. McCurry, the President's press secretary, that "there are no chances at this point" of President Clinton signing legislation that would prevent the Government from coming to a screeching halt next week.

That prompted the Republican leaders, Speaker Newt Gingrich and Senator Bob Dole, to call a news conference at the Capitol where they sought to assign blame for the conflict to the White House.

"It is very difficult to work with a President who seems to be primarily driven by his political advisers to engage in public relations stunts," Mr. Gingrich said.

And Mr. Dole said: "It's up to the President of the United States. If the Government shuts down, his fingerprints are going to be all over it."

Not to be outdone, Treasury Secretary Robert E. Rubin and Leon E. Panetta, the President's chief of staff, scurried to the White House press room.

"Don't put a gun to the head of the President and the head of the country," said Mr. Panetta. "That's a form of terrorism."

Mr. Panetta held out the prospect of 800,000 Federal employees being furloughed on Tuesday. The President summoned his Cabinet to the White House to outline the process of boarding up the Government if money runs out.

Mr. Rubin released a letter to Mr. Gingrich from six former Treasury secretaries, four Democrats and two Republicans, imploring the Speaker not to let political and policy differences over the budget impede the Government's orderly access to credit markets.

This led Mr. Gingrich, Mr. Dole and other Republican leaders to send a public letter to the President, saying that "despite the inflammatory and highly partisan rhetoric that continues to flow from your White House staff," Republicans would like to work with Mr. Clinton to enact a balanced budget within seven years.

"Instead of meeting with your Cabinet to plan a Government shutdown," the leaders wrote, "you should be meeting with the leadership of Congress to devise a plan to keep the Government operating while we work together on a balanced budget."

This is the situation that led to the political crossfire: Only two of the 13 appropriations bills have been enacted to provide money for Government departments and agencies in the fiscal year that began Oct. 1. A temporary spending bill to breach the gap expires at midnight Monday. If spending authority is not extended, the Government will have to close down except for emergency services.

Meanwhile, the Treasury is butting against the $4.9 billion statutory limit on how much money it can borrow. Republicans want to place a higher debt ceiling in the big budget bill now pending in a Senate-House conference to make it harder for the President to veto the measure.

But the overall budget bill is at least weeks away from enactment. If the debt ceiling is not raised, however, the Treasury may not have enough money to meet interest payments due next week.

Similar situations have been reached in years past. Each side would try to get the other to blink. And when neither would do so, they would eventually blink in unison.

But that was when Democrats controlled Congress and Republicans the White House. That lineup is now reversed. So the outcome cannot safely be predicted based on what happened in the past.

On Wednesday night, the House passed a measure extending the Government's spending authority through Dec. 1. But it tacked on extraneous material, including a measure prohibiting organizations that receive Federal grants from lobbying the Government or otherwise engaging in political advocacy. Another provision added would set Medicare premiums paid by the elderly higher than they would be without a change in the law.

Today, by a vote of 227 to 194 that essentially followed party lines, the House then passed another bill raising the debt ceiling enough to get the Government through mid-December. But it added more riders to this bill, including measures that would abolish the Commerce Department, limit the appeals of convicts on death row and place restrictions on Government regulations dealing with the environment and other matters.

These extraneous riders were apparently necessary to get the temporary spending bill and debt limit extension past conservative Republicans in the House. But they are opposed not just by President Clinton but by many in the Senate.

The main controversy in the temporary spending bill involved the prohibition on lobbying by organizations receiving Federal grants. The Senate debated the matter all day and finally passed, 49 to 47, a watered-down version of what the House had approved.

The changes won over a group of moderate Republicans who rigorously opposed the language as it was passed by the House. In the end, only three Republicans -- James M. Jeffords of Vermont, Arlen Specter of Pennsylvania and Olympia J. Snowe of Maine -- joined the Democrats in opposing the measure.

Senator Alan K. Simpson, Republican of Wyoming, implored his colleagues to vote for the restriction on lobbying because it was so important to conservatives in the House. Its defeat, he declared, would "create a most horrendous reaction in the House."

But Senator Bob Kerrey, Democrat of Nebraska, dismissed that argument. "You have a minority in the House," he said, "that says 'I'm going to hold my breath until I get my way.' "

The debate in the House on the debt legislation can be summarized by this exchange:

Representative Richard J. Durbin, Democrat of Illinois: "It's the kind of political game that gives politics a bad name."

Representative Scott McInnis, Republican of Colorado: "Talk about the children of the next generation -- that's where the impact is."

Meantime, an impasse over an abortion measure stymied Senate and House negotiators trying to work out differences on a $243 billion military spending bill for the current fiscal year.

The House favors a ban on abortions at United States military hospitals. The Senate negotiators oppose such a measure.

Written Testimony of
Jacob J. Lew
Secretary of the Treasury
Before the Senate Committee on Finance
October 10, 2013

Introduction

Chairman Baucus, Ranking Member Hatch, and members of the Committee, thank you for inviting me here today to discuss the potential impacts of a failure by Congress to increase the debt ceiling. This is an important moment in American history, and Congress has an important choice to make for the American people. Congress alone has the power to act to make sure that the full faith and credit of the United States is never called into question. No Congress in 224 years of American history has allowed our country to default, and it is my sincere hope that this Congress will not be the first. At the same time, Congress should pass legislation to fund the government and end the standoff.

State of U.S. Economy and Fiscal Position

Since February 2010, private employers have added about 7 and a half million jobs, and over the last year alone they added more than 2 million jobs. Manufacturing is expanding while the housing market continues to improve, posting gains in sales, prices, and residential construction.

At the same time, we have been working with Congress to achieve a sustainable fiscal path. In its most recent estimates, the Congressional Budget Office projected that the 2013 deficit would be less than half the more than 9 percent of GDP deficit the President inherited. The rapid deficit reduction of the past two years is the result of both a stronger economy and the deficit reduction that the President has already signed into law.

Among the risks that we control, the biggest threat to sustained growth in our economy is the recurrence of manufactured crises in Washington and self-inflicted wounds. Unfortunately, we now face a manufactured political crisis that is beginning to deliver an unnecessary blow to our economy – right at a time when the U.S. economy and the American people have painstakingly fought back from the worst recession since the Great Depression.

Private-sector economists have estimated that a two-week government shutdown could directly reduce real GDP growth in the fourth quarter by about a quarter percentage point at an annual rate. Some have warned that a longer shutdown would reduce economic growth as much as 1½ percentage points. These estimates typically do not include the additional spillovers that seem likely: household and business confidence in the government could fall sharply, and other spending that relies on a functioning federal government could be postponed or cancelled. Why would anyone want to do that to our economy?

In addition to the economic cost of the shutdown, the uncertainty around raising the debt limit is beginning to stress the financial markets. Yields on Treasury bills maturing in the second half of

October and early November have already surpassed the peaks on similarly affected maturities in July 2011. At our auction of four-week Treasury bills on Tuesday, the interest rate nearly tripled relative to the prior week's auction and reached the highest level since Oct 2008. Measures of expected volatility in the stock market have risen to the highest levels of the year.

The only way to avoid further self-inflicted wounds to our economy is for Congress to act. I know from my conversations with a wide range of business leaders representing industries from retail to manufacturing to banking that this is a paramount concern for them. That is why it is important for Congress to reopen the government and raise the debt ceiling, and then to work with the President to address our long-term fiscal challenges in a balanced and thoughtful way.

Potential Economic Impact of Failure to Raise the Debt Limit

The Treasury Department recently released a report examining the potential macroeconomic effects of political brinksmanship in 2011, and the potential risks of waiting until the last possible moment to increase the debt limit in the current economic environment. It points to the potentially catastrophic impacts of default, including credit market disruptions, a significant loss in the value of the dollar, markedly elevated U.S. interest rates, negative spillover effects to the global economy, and real risk of a financial crisis and recession that could echo the events of 2008 or worse.

If interest rates rose, it would have a real impact on American households. The stock market, including investments in retirement accounts, could tumble, and it could become more expensive for Americans to buy a car, own a home, and open a small business.

These additional costs of borrowing could not easily be undone and our actions would impact Americans for generations to come.

Failing to raise the debt ceiling will impact everyday Americans beyond its impact on financial markets. For example, doctors receiving reimbursements under Medicare would likely continue to provide services on a timely basis, but they would be operating with significant uncertainty about when they would be paid by the government for their services. For millions of low-income Americans who rely on Medicaid for their healthcare, the federal government's payments to states for the federal contribution would likely also be impacted. These providers still have to pay their doctors, nurses, and staff, but absent timely federal payments, many could face real liquidity challenges. And for those waiting on benefits who need those funds in order to refill their refrigerator – if that money doesn't flow, they won't go to the grocery store to shop, creating ripple effects that would be felt throughout the economy. The bottom line is that failing to raise the debt ceiling creates a very difficult and unfair situation, and one that is completely avoidable if Congress acts.

It is also important to note that the federal government has numerous large payments that are due shortly after October 17, when we will have exhausted our borrowing authority and will only have cash on hand to meet our obligations. Between October 17 and November 1, we have large payments to Medicare providers, Social Security beneficiaries, and veterans, as well as salaries for active duty members of the military. A failure to raise the debt limit could put timely payment of all of these at risk.

We need to look no further than 2011 for evidence of what just an extended debate on the merits of raising the debt limit can do to our economy. In 2011, U.S. government debt was downgraded for the first time in history, the stock market fell, measures of volatility jumped, and credit risk spreads widened noticeably; these financial market effects persisted for months. To be sure, other forces both at home and abroad also played a role, but the uncertainty surrounding whether or not the U.S. government would pay its bills had a lasting impact on both markets and the economy.

History of Bipartisan Support for Increasing the Debt Limit

Republican and Democratic Presidents and Treasury Secretaries alike have universally understood the importance of protecting one of our most precious assets – the full faith and credit of the United States. President Reagan wrote to Congress in 1983: "This country now possesses the strongest credit in the world. The full consequences of a default – or even the serious prospect of default – by the United States are impossible to predict and awesome to contemplate. Denigration of the full faith and credit of the United States would have substantial effects on the domestic financial markets and on the value of the dollar in exchange markets."

Employers across the country also understand the importance of what is at stake if we default on our debts for the first time in American history. Last week, 251 business organizations, including the Chamber of Commerce, National Association of Manufacturers, and National Retail Federation wrote in a letter to Congress: "We urge Congress to act promptly to pass a Continuing Resolution to fund the government and to raise the debt ceiling, and then to return to work on these other vital issues."

No credible economist or business leader thinks that defaulting is good for job creation or economic growth. Henry Paulson, Treasury Secretary under President George W. Bush, said last month, "it is unthinkable that Congress wouldn't live up to our commitment to make good on past spending commitments and obligations." Chairman of the Federal Reserve Ben Bernanke said recently, "a failure to raise the debt limit could have very serious consequences for the financial markets and for the economy." And Warren Buffett said last week that "it makes absolutely no sense" for some in Congress to use the debt ceiling as leverage, saying "it ought to be banned as a weapon . . . . It should be like nuclear bombs, basically too horrible to use." They understand that Congress choosing not to pay the government's bills is unacceptable and could do irrevocable harm to our economy.

If Congress fails to meet its responsibility, it could be deeply damaging to the financial markets, the ongoing economic recovery, and the jobs and savings of millions of Americans. I have a responsibility to be transparent with the American people about these risks. And I think it would be a grave mistake to discount or dismiss them. For these reasons, I have repeatedly urged Congress to take action immediately so we can honor all of the country's past commitments.

James Baker, Treasury Secretary under President Reagan, made this point to Congress in 1987, saying, "Running out of cash means that the United States would default on its obligations both domestic and foreign, with all the negative financial, legal and moral consequences that implies. Our Founding Fathers regarded the full faith and credit of the United States as a sacred trust, and for over 200 years the United States has upheld this fiduciary duty. The United States has never defaulted on its debt obligations. To do so would be unthinkable and irresponsible. We would seriously erode this country's premier credit position and break faith with our citizens."

Treasury's Communication with Congress

Earlier this year, Congress enacted the No Budget No Pay Act that increased the debt ceiling through May 18. Upon reaching that date, Treasury began using what are called extraordinary measures to avoid defaulting on our obligations. The Treasury Department has been open and transparent, regularly updating Congress over the course of the last five months as new information has become available about when we would exhaust our extraordinary measures. In addition, Treasury has provided information about what our cash balances will be when we exhaust our extraordinary measures. As our forecasts have changed, I have consistently updated Congress in order to give Congress the best information about the urgency with which they should act. And last month, I met with the full membership of this committee to discuss these issues.

On August 26, I notified Congress that these extraordinary measures would be exhausted by the middle of October, and that I anticipated a cash balance of roughly $50 billion at the point of exhaustion. On September 25, I wrote to Congress again to notify that, due to lower-than-expected quarterly revenue collections and changes in the size and timing of certain large trust fund transactions, we then projected that extraordinary measures would be exhausted no later than October 17, and that our remaining cash balance would be closer to $30 billion. Most recently, just last week, I sent a letter to Congress that said, as of October 1, Treasury has begun using the final extraordinary measures. There are no other legal and prudent options to extend the nation's borrowing authority and provide Congress with more time to act.

Treasury continues to believe that extraordinary measures will be exhausted no later than October 17, 2013, at which point the federal government will have run out of borrowing authority. At that point we will be left to meet our country's commitments with only the cash on hand and any incoming revenues, placing our economy in a dangerous position. We will continue to monitor the impact of the protracted government shutdown on revenues and expenditures. If we have insufficient cash on hand, it would be impossible for the United States of America to meet all of its obligations – including Social Security and Medicare benefits, payments to our military and veterans, and contracts with private suppliers – for the first time in our history. At the same time, we are relying on investors from all over the world to continue to hold U.S. bonds. Every week, we roll-over approximately $100 billion in U.S. bills. If U.S. bond holders decided that they wanted to be repaid rather than continuing to roll-over their Treasury investments, we could unexpectedly dissipate our entire cash balance.

Let me be clear. Trying to time a debt limit increase to the last minute could be very dangerous. If Congress does not act and the U.S. suddenly cannot pay its bills, the repercussions would be serious.

Irresponsible Arguments Against Raising the Debt Limit

Raising the debt limit is Congress's responsibility because Congress, and Congress alone, is empowered to set the maximum amount the government can borrow to meet its financial obligations.

Some in Congress have suggested that raising the debt limit should be paired with accompanying spending cuts and reforms. I have repeatedly noted that the debt limit has nothing to do with new spending. It has to do with spending that Congress has already approved and bills that have already been incurred. Failing to raise the debt limit would not make these bills disappear. The President remains willing to negotiate over the future direction of fiscal policy, but he will not negotiate over whether the United States should pay its bills.

Certain members of the House and Senate believe that it is possible to protect our economy by simply paying only the interest on our debts, while stopping or delaying payments on a number of our other legal commitments. The United States should not be put in a position of making such perilous choices for our economy and our citizens. There is no way of knowing the irrevocable damage such an approach would have on our economy and financial markets.

As administrations of both political parties have previously determined, these "prioritization" proposals do not solve the problem. They represent an irresponsible retreat from a core American value: since 1789, regardless of party, Presidents and Congress have always honored all of our commitments. We cannot afford for Congress to gamble with the full faith and credit of the United States of America. At the same time, we should never be put in a position where we have to pick which commitments our nation should meet. How can the United States choose whether to send Social Security checks to seniors or pay benefits to our veterans? How can the United States choose whether to provide children with food assistance or meet our obligations to Medicare providers?

Rational decisions require assessing abstract risks – the alternative is trial and error. We are seeing with the government shutdown how those that denied there would be any impact are struggling every day to address real consequences with patches. This does not work. They need to open the government.

It is irresponsible and reckless to insist that we experience a forced default to learn how bad it is. If anything at all is learned from the shutdown, it will convince the deniers – or a majority who can work their will – to avoid putting the entire economy at risk in the name of an ideological fight.

There is a suggestion by some in Congress that the debt limit has traditionally been used as a tool to address budgetary and fiscal issues. This is not historically accurate. Since World War II, Congress has routinely raised the debt limit through standalone legislation signed by both

Democratic and Republican Presidents. Since President Reagan was inaugurated in 1981, Congress has enacted 45 different pieces of legislation to raise, extend, or revise the definition of the debt limit.

According to the Center on Budget and Policy Priorities, between 1981 and 2011, policymakers enacted nine bipartisan deficit reduction packages. Only three of those legislative packages also included debt limit increases:

- The Gramm-Rudman-Hollings budget compromises in 1985 and 1986;
- The Budget Enforcement Act in 1990; and
- The Balanced Budget Act in 1997.

In each of these three instances, the debate was driven by fiscal policy and how to achieve deficit reduction in a responsible, balanced manner. Neither political party thought that defaulting on our debt was a serious, credible option. In 1985, the need to raise the debt limit served as a deadline for budget negotiations. In 1990, Congress and the President worked together to avoid across-the-board cuts from the original Gramm-Rudman sequestration, which were universally viewed as the wrong way to reduce the deficit. In 1997, Congress added a debt limit increase at the end of negotiations, after the parties agreed on a deal to reduce the deficit responsibly and grow the economy. I participated personally in many of these negotiations, and I do not recall anyone ever seriously suggesting that the United States should fail to pay its bills.

The summer of 2011 was different. Certain Members of Congress argued that default was an acceptable outcome if they were unable to achieve their legislative objectives. Rather than enter into a good-faith compromise on fiscal issues, these Members argued that the United States should voluntarily fail to pay its bills if their position was not accepted. Our economy paid a significant price for these irresponsible and protracted threats. The full faith and credit of the United States is not a bargaining chip. It is reckless and irresponsible to put our full faith and credit at risk.

The President has been and is willing to negotiate over the future direction of long-term fiscal policy. He has repeatedly proposed a comprehensive and balanced package of deficit reduction proposals. And that is why he proposed a budget that reflects the difficult choices he believes we need to make as a country. Within that budget, the President included entitlement reforms, unpopular with many Democrats, and tax reform that would spur economic growth and cut our deficit. And he has made it absolutely clear that he is ready to sit down with Republicans and Democrats to find common ground. The House and Senate have each passed their own budgets, and on 18 separate occasions the Senate Budget Committee Chair has requested that a conference committee be convened so both sides can negotiate and iron out their differences. But Republicans have refused each of those requests. And so instead of negotiating a budget deal over the last 6 months, as Democrats have requested, we now find ourselves on the precipice with some Republicans once again threatening default.

Conclusion

Leaders have a responsibility to make our economy stronger, not to create manufactured crises that inflict damage. The very last thing we need now is a fight over whether we raise the debt ceiling. Not when we face serious challenges both domestically and internationally that require our full attention. And not when we know the kind of damage a financial and economic crisis can cause.

A great democracy does not lurch from one self-inflicted crisis to another. The time for discussions around the fiscal choices we need to make should not take place after we shut down the government or in the last seconds before a default. The time for these discussions is during the normal budget process. This is a stand that Democratic and Republican Presidents must take to make clear that under no circumstances will the United States fail to pay our bills.

I will close by noting that as we meet today, finance ministers from all over the world are gathered in Washington for the IMF and World Bank annual meetings, and it's worth taking a moment to recognize that our country has special role in global financial markets. The United States is the anchor of the international financial system. It is the world's largest economy with the deepest and most liquid financial markets. When risk rises, the flight to safety and to quality brings investors to U.S. markets. Other countries look to us for how to govern and how to maintain economic vitality. The United States cannot take this hard-earned reputation for granted. We have spent 224 years building the nation's credit as the strongest in the world, and only Congress can act to protect it. A default for the first time in our history could pose serious risks to our global standing.

The simple truth is Congress must get this done. The time to do it is now before any more damage is done to the U.S. economy.

Questions for the Record for Secretary Lew

From the 10/10/2013 hearing of the Senate Committee on Finance titled "The Debt Limit"

From Senator Orrin Hatch

1. I have expressed my disappointment over administration officials publicly questioning sentiments of Americans and financial market participants and suggesting that people are being too calm. The administration and others have also made clear their fear of catastrophic consequences should the United States fail to pay an incoming due obligation. The view of the administration is that the debt limit impasse poses an emerging risk to the stability of the financial system and the economy. Administration officials have also publicly questioned their abilities to ensure timely payments to seniors and disabled American workers in the Social Security programs.

   Of course, no one wants a default of any kind. And I will do everything I possibly can to prevent such a thing, and I do not believe a default would ever happen. But statements from you and other administration officials suggest that you fear such an outcome. From a risk management perspective, you therefore must have contingency plans. Put simply, hope that the unthinkable could never happen is not a plan.

   A) Given your fear of an emerging risk from the debt limit, will you use your discretion to extend the debt issuance suspension period? If not, why not?

The Secretary of the Treasury does not have unlimited discretion to declare a debt issuance suspension period. Under the relevant statute, the term "debt issuance suspension period" means the period of time that the Treasury Secretary determines that Treasury securities cannot be issued without exceeding the debt limit. The determination of the length of the period must be based on the facts as they exist at the time.

   B) As Managing Trustee of the Social Security Trust Funds, what plans do you have to protect seniors and disabled American workers if the catastrophic outcome that you fear were to be realized?

The only way to protect seniors, disabled American workers, and other Americans from very serious harm was for Congress to extend the nation's borrowing authority.

   C) As the Chair of the Financial Stability Oversight Council, which is charged with the responsibility of monitoring emerging threats to financial stability, does the Council intend to issue any warnings of an emerging threat and do you and other members of the Council have contingency plans to share with Americans? If not, why not?

As early as July 2011, in its first annual report to Congress, the Council stated, "It is vital to the stability of the U.S. financial system and the global financial system for the debt limit to be raised in a timely manner to avoid creating any risk of default on U.S. obligations." The Council's 2012 and 2013 annual reports both discussed the significant repercussions of any failure to raise the debt limit. The Council will continue to monitor potential risks related to the debt limit as appropriate.

    D) As Treasury Secretary, do you have any plans for how you would confront a debt limit crisis, such as preserving principle and interest payments through Fedwire while bundling payments made to others through automated clearing houses?

As in the past, Treasury staff considered a range of options with respect to how Treasury would operate if the United States had exhausted its borrowing authority. Ultimately, the decision of how Treasury would have operated would have been made by the President. Because Congress acted in time, no such decision was necessary.

2. Please provide Treasury's operating cash balance projections for a period between your receipt of this question and the date at which you choose to respond to this question (which should be within 30 days of receipt of the question). For each day within that period, provide Treasury's projection of its operating cash balance for the following business day and each business day thereafter for up to seven days. For example, report the projection made on October 16 for the operating cash balance of October 17, 19, 21, 22, 23, 24, and 25. Congress and the American people need to know about Treasury's cash and debt management operations, and knowledge of these projections will help. Please, also, retain records of Treasury's internal forecasts of future operating cash balances, along with any accompanying data, so that members of the Senate Finance Committee and others can, as part of their oversight responsibilities, review Treasury's projection techniques and forecasting performance.

As we have said numerous times in our communications with Congress, there is inherent variability in the projection of our cash balance on any given day. The 16-day government shutdown further increased the complexity and variability of cash balance projections. As explained in our September 25 letter to Congress, and reiterated in our October 1 letter, we expected that extraordinary measures would be exhausted no later than October 17, and at that time we would be left to meet our obligations with roughly $30 billion. As found in the Daily Treasury Statement (http://www.fms.treas.gov/dts/index.html), the closing cash balance on October 16, the day Congress acted to raise the debt ceiling, was $31.866 billion, and $46.296 billion on October 17. Our internal projections were similar to those numbers.

3. Some participants in markets for Treasury securities have recently identified their belief that market participants have prepared, operationally, to deal with a contingency in which Treasury fails to make a timely payment on a security. Given settlement and processing of daily transactions in Treasury securities found within Fedwire, the clearing banks, DTCC,

and the triparty repo market, for example, it has also been identified that to enhance functioning of the settlement infrastructure, early notice to the market of any Treasury intent to extend a payment date would be helpful, should the unlikely event of payment extension, that no one wants to have happen, was to occur. Some market participants, including some that serve on the Treasury Borrowing Advisory Committee, have also reported an understanding that, in the unlikely event that Treasury found itself unable to make a timely payment on interest or principal on a Treasury security, "Treasury will determine payments/postponements on a day by day basis."

A) In the unlikely, though thinkable, event of an inability to make a timely payment on interest or principal on a Treasury security, would Treasury provide advance notice of a failure to pay on Treasury securities?

B) Have any market participants been told that such advance notice would occur?

C) Has anyone at the Treasury Department made statements publicly, or to any member(s) of its Borrowing Advisory Committee, identifying that in the event of an inability to make timely payments on interest or principal on a Treasury security, Treasury will determine payments/postponements on a day by day basis? If so, has the information been made available to anyone in Congress? And if no such statements have been made, do financial market participants have an incorrect understanding?

The following answer responds to questions A - C.

No decisions have been made about how we would manage in an environment in which we were unable to make a timely payment on a Treasury security. Treasury has always maintained that default is unthinkable and Congress must do its job to preserve the full faith and credit of the United States. In addition, we note that the minutes of TBAC meetings are publicly released.

From Senator Enzi

1. You have discussed the significant economic consequences of not raising the debt limit. However, the Administration has not always been as forthright about analyzing the economic impact of its own actions. For example, the President's health care law included a number of new taxes. One of these taxes is a premium sales tax imposed upon health insurance providers. The Administration, in the proposed rule, noted that this rule was not a "significant" rulemaking action with an adverse impact upon the economy of $100 million or more. However, recent data on the amount collected by the tax as well as the pass-through costs resulting from this tax appear to show that this assessment may not have been based on all available data. Representative Paulsen and I, along with a number of our colleagues, sent a letter to you and the acting IRS commissioner on this issue. We have requested a response by October 18. Will the Treasury Department and the IRS meet this deadline for a response? If not, why not?

2. As part of its calculations, did the Administration account for the pass-through costs of the tax to families and small businesses in the form of higher insurance premiums and to states through higher Medicaid costs? If not, why not?

3. Did the Administration calculate the economic impact of the pass-through costs imposed as a result of this tax, including lost wages, reduced health benefits and employment opportunities? If not, why not?

The following answer responds to questions 1-3.

Section 9010 of the ACA imposes an allocated fee on entities engaged in the business of providing health insurance. The aggregate amount of the annual fee to be paid by the health insurance providers is set forth in the statute. The proposed regulations, which were released in March 2013, provide clarity as to which types of coverage are considered health insurance for purposes of the fee and define certain terms used in the statute. In addition, the regulations provide rules for reporting and paying the fee, and outline an error correction process for use by health insurance providers after reviewing an initial fee calculation generated by the Internal Revenue Service.

You raise questions about the application of Executive Order 12866 to the proposed regulations. Pursuant to Office of Management and Budget (OMB) guidance and longstanding agreements between OMB and Treasury, only IRS legislative rules that constitute "significant regulatory actions" are subject to Executive Order 12866 review. Thus, pursuant to longstanding practice across several Administrations, most IRS rules, including the proposed regulations, are not subject to E.O. 12866 review.

We are carefully considering all comments we receive on the proposed regulations, and we intend to continue to work with health insurance providers as the fee is implemented.

From Senator Thune

1) Two years ago, your predecessor, Timothy Geithner, testified before the Senate Budget Committee that countries with a debt-to-GDP ratio generally experience slower economic growth. Do you agree with that conclusion? Likewise, do you believe that reducing our debt-to-GDP ratio over the long run will generally lead to greater economic growth? If one or both of those are the case, will the administration work with Congress to reduce our unsustainable budget deficits?

Academic research has generally shown a correlation between countries with high debt-to-GDP ratios and slower economic growth. However, more recent research has called into question the direction of causality, and acknowledged the possibility that slower growth leads to higher debt, not vice versa. Moreover, it appears from the available data that the different circumstances that different countries face matter significantly, and there is not a specific or universal debt-to-GDP tipping point beyond which debt begins to impact economic growth.

The relationship between the debt-to-GDP ratio and economic growth over various time horizons is not straightforward. Although it is clear that we need to ensure a long-run sustainable path for our debt, it seems equally clear that rapid fiscal contraction has had a negative impact on jobs and growth over the last several years, and continuing on this path puts at risk full economic recovery and a timely return to full employment. The Administration remains committed to working with Congress to promote fiscal sustainability. The President supports a balanced approach to deficit reduction, replacing the indiscriminate cuts of the sequester with a deficit-reduction plan that is supportive of both near-term economic recovery and long-term fiscal sustainability. Such a balanced approach requires consideration of both the composition and the timing of fiscal consolidation, and would draw upon both spending cuts and revenue increases as well as protections for the most vulnerable Americans.

2) Do you agree with the Congressional Budget Office that increased borrowing by the federal government will reduce private investment, lower output and income, and increase the risk of a fiscal crisis? If so, as Congress agrees to raise the debt ceiling by another $1 trillion wouldn't it be the "responsible" action to at least have a conversation about reducing our debt _before_ the debt limit is increased?

It is my understanding that the Congressional Budget Office (CBO) generally does not believe that all federal government borrowing automatically or necessarily reduces private investment or lowers output and income. I agree with CBO that the composition and timing of federal government expenditures, including expenditures financed through borrowing, leads to a range of consequences for aggregate output. In some cases, changes in federal government outlays – for instance, tax expenditures targeted toward higher-income households – can lead to proportionally smaller changes in aggregate output and private investment. However, in other cases, changes in federal government outlays can lead to proportionally larger changes in aggregate output and private investment. The overall effect depends on several factors, including how the proceeds of the borrowing are used, whether there are unused resources in the economy, and the monetary policy response.

The President has been clear that he is committed to negotiation about all aspects of fiscal policy, but not about raising the debt limit. Raising the debt limit is not about authorizing new spending, but about ensuring that the country fulfills its commitment for spending decisions that have already been made. The Administration is eager to engage in a constructive conversation about the country's long-term fiscal challenges. However, as demonstrated this October, doing so under the threat of default results in unnecessary macroeconomic volatility and erodes confidence among investors, business, and consumers.

3) The president has continued to say that he agrees we need to address the true drivers of our long-term debt. However, after five debt limit increases, we have seen very little evidence to suggest his comments are more than talking points. What assurances can you give to the members of this Committee that you will act in good faith in the short-term to negotiate entitlement reforms?

The Administration believes we have made great progress reducing the deficit over the past three years. Thanks to actions taken by Congress and the Administration since January 2011 that both cut spending and raised revenue, deficits over the next decade have been reduced by more than $2.5 trillion. The federal deficit is now half of what it was as a share of the economy when the President took office, and it is falling at the fastest pace over a sustained period since World War II.

The President has been and continues to be willing to work with Congress to make the difficult choices necessary to ensure the long-run sustainability of the federal budget, including our entitlement programs. The President's FY 2014 Budget contains numerous reforms to both health and non-health entitlement programs, many of which are also found in bipartisan proposals that have been released in the past few years as well as individual proposals from members of both parties.

4) If Congress were able to agree upon a short term agreement on a CR and debt limit suspension, would the administration be willing to negotiate meaningful changes to our entitlement programs that would put our country on a more stable financial footing?

The President has repeatedly expressed his willingness to work with anyone on entitlement reform that puts our country on a more stable financial footing. The President's own FY 2014 budget reflects his willingness to confront the financing challenges of our entitlement programs.

5) If Congress were able to agree upon a short term agreement on a CR and debt limit suspension, would the administration be willing to negotiate bipartisan changes to ObamaCare as part of a plan to reform entitlement programs?

The President is always open to discussing good faith ideas for making the Affordable Care Act more helpful and cost-effective to the American people; however, he is not open to proposals that undermine the fundamentals of the law.

6) Mr. Secretary, the President has stated on a number of occasions his desire for Republicans to agree to yet another tax increase before the Administration will agree to discuss entitlement reforms, even those entitlement reforms in the President's own budget. As you know, last month the CBO updated their long term outlook and it shows that federal revenues will be back up to their historical 50-year average of nearly 18 percent by next year and will be 18.6 percent of GDP by 2015, without any new tax increase whatsoever. CBO projects taxes as a share of the economy will stay above the historical norm throughout the next ten years – again, without any new tax increases. Why does the administration continue to insist on tax increases as a prerequisite for any deficit reduction package? How much higher than the "normal" level of taxation does the Administration seek? 20 percent of GDP; 25 percent of GDP; 30 percent of GDP?

The Administration and virtually every bipartisan fiscal commission over the past three years have advocated for a balanced approach to deficit reduction that includes reductions in spending along with additional revenue. That balance needs to reflect both the level of spending and revenues as well as their composition. Revenues as a share of the GDP remain below their share in 2000 (when the federal budget was in surplus), prior to the enactment of temporary tax cuts in 2001. Moreover, a long-term average of historic revenues does not necessarily inform us about the appropriate level of revenues in the future. The population has grown and changed significantly over the past 40 years, and will continue to grow and change; the functions performed by the federal government also continue to change. Fifty years ago, Medicare had not yet been enacted, and the level of sophistication and cost of our military investments was very different than it is today.

Finally, note that earlier this year, the American Taxpayer Relief Act locked in marginal individual income tax rates at 1990s levels for high-income households, and at or below 1990s levels for the rest of Americans. The President's Budget calls for comprehensive tax reform that cuts tax expenditures and uses the revenue to further lower rates and reduce deficits.

Senator John D. Rockefeller IV

Statement for the Record

"The Debt Limit"

October 10, 2013

Mr. Chairman, I appreciate that you called this hearing today to highlight a critically important topic. I also want to thank Secretary Lew for making the time to be here, during what I know is a very busy time.

I regret that we have to be here today to talk about the consequences of failing to raise the debt ceiling. I am sorry that we have to even think about the consequences of inaction. Failing to raise the debt ceiling will hurt all West Virginians and all Americans. Defaulting on our debt could lead to interruptions in Social Security and veterans benefits. It could lead to increased interest rates when families buy a home or car. Pension funds and retirement accounts could see their values plummet.

Earlier this week, the President said that America should not have to pay a ransom in exchange for the authority to pay its bills. I agree. What's happening here in Congress is reckless behavior. The very fabric of our economy that we've worked so hard to fix after the recession is being threatened in a selfish effort to push unrelated policies and political agendas.

I cannot fathom how we have reached this place, where elected men and women are willfully putting the economic security of their own constituents at serious risk. Last week, those who are blocking government funding said it was because of Obamacare. This week, that rationale has fallen apart, so they flail around for other excuses. We have sent the House a clean CR and over the next week we will aim to send them a clean debt limit increase. The CR has the votes to pass if only Speaker Boehner, who controls the floor, would allow it to come before the full body. The clean debt limit I suspect could also pass, but I fear it will be subject to the same efforts of obstruction.

It is technically true that we can't say for sure what the consequences will be if we do not raise the debt limit. But that is because we have never been foolish enough to consider default. Today, the expert predictions of nearly every leading economist are that a failure to raise the debt ceiling will weaken the economy, hurt American jobs and retirement savings, and raise interest rates on loans and credit cards.

The U.S. Treasury says it could plunge our economy back into a recession as dire as the recession caused by the collapse of the financial markets in 2008. That is frightening. We all remember vividly the very personal impacts of the recession. Some people are still dealing with the economic fallout. Some may deal with it for the rest of their lives.

We heard countless stories of people who had been employed their entire lives who lost their job and what they went through psychologically when they had to apply for unemployment. We all knew people in our communities who sacrificed so much of their savings just so their children could eat and have health care. We watched as people lost their lifelong homes, businesses they built from scratch, and their hard-earned retirement savings. And we heard heartbreaking stories about parents who had to tell their college students they could no longer pay for the education they dreamed of. I can't imagine anyone wanting to relive that. So I find it unconscionable that some here in Congress see no problem with taking more unnecessary risks that could again devastate our economy as a whole.

Congress has raised the debt ceiling twelve times since 2001 under both Democratic and Republican Presidents. It is a routine matter for the Congress because it simply ensures the United States pays for the debts that we have already incurred under laws previously approved by the Congress. The time for great debate is when we are enacting the laws that spend taxpayer money, not after the debt comes due for the money already lawfully spent.

None of us sitting up here would advise our family, our friends, or our constituents to stop paying their debts. We know that is ludicrous advice. But today there are some Members of Congress who are so obsessed with repealing the Affordable Care Act, and crippling government and the countless services it provides to the American people, that they are pushing a dangerous misinformation campaign and making light of the implications of default. I believe that these people have no regard for our economy's health. I also believe they have no regard for the long-term economic security of their constituents. These reckless efforts, which they try to veil as attempts to curb government spending, are deeply misguided and put our country, and the global economy, in jeopardy.

Furthermore, we have already enacted major spending cuts. The fiscal cliff deal enacted January 1 of this year took strong steps to reduce the deficit and restore our fiscal solvency, in part by making more than $2 trillion in budget cuts. Many of these cuts were truly hard on West Virginians. Essential services, including housing and nutrition that so many West Virginia families need, were cut back. So I do not want to hear from anyone that the sequester happened and no one got hurt. That is not true.

In recent budget negotiations, Senate Democrats accepted budget cuts requested by House Republicans. The continuing resolution we passed, and that Speaker Boehner refuses to bring to a vote in the House, locks in these painful cuts for another year. House Republicans say they want more, but they cannot articulate what more they want.

At the beginning of this Congress, then-Treasury Secretary Geithner wrote to Congressional leadership. He shared the following quote from Ronald Reagan, with the hope that my Republican colleagues would especially take heed.

In 1987, President Reagan said, "Unfortunately, Congress consistently brings us to the edge of default before facing its responsibility. This brinkmanship threatens the holders of government bonds and those who rely on Social Security and veterans benefits. Interest rates would skyrocket. Instability would occur in financial markets and the federal deficit would soar. The United States has a special responsibility to itself and the world to meet its obligations. It means we have a well-earned reputation for reliability and credibility – two things that set us apart in much of the world."

If my colleagues won't listen to my arguments for why we should raise the debt ceiling, I do hope they listen to President Reagan's.

NATIONAL ASSOCIATION OF
Manufacturers

Jay Timmons
President and CEO

October 8, 2013

The President
The White House
Washington, DC 20500

The Honorable John Boehner
Speaker of the House
United States House of Representatives
Washington, DC 20515

The Honorable Nancy Pelosi
Minority Leader
United States House of Representatives
Washington, DC 20515

The Honorable Harry Reid
Majority Leader
United States Senate
Washington, DC 20510

The Honorable Mitch McConnell
Minority Leader
United States Senate
Washington, DC 20510

Dear Mr. President, Speaker Boehner and Leaders Pelosi, Reid and McConnell:

On behalf of the National Association of Manufacturers (NAM)—the largest manufacturing association in the United States, representing small and large manufacturers in every industrial sector and in all 50 states—I write to strongly urge you to act as soon as possible to raise the statutory debt limit.

The failure of policymakers to address this critical issue is injecting uncertainty in the U.S. economy, hampering the ability of manufacturers and the broader business community to compete, invest and create new jobs. In a recent survey of NAM members, almost two-thirds of respondents said it is extremely important for the President and Congress to make progress on funding the government for fiscal year 2014 and extending the nation's debt ceiling. More than 90 percent said that addressing the nation's fiscal challenges was important for their company.

Manufacturers believe the United States must meet our financial obligations to ensure global investors' continuing confidence in the nation's creditworthiness. Our nation has never defaulted in the past, and failing to raise the debt limit in a timely fashion will seriously disrupt our fragile economy and have a ripple effect throughout the world. In particular, a default would put upward pressure on interest rates, raising both the short- and long-term cost of capital and discouraging business investment and job creation. In addition, a default would create an uncertain fiscal environment that will discourage foreign direct investment in the United States that could harm our economy for years to come.

Our nation's economic future depends on your actions. Now is the time to rise above partisan differences and put the nation's best interests first by addressing the debt limit. Thank you in advance for the leadership that will be necessary to appropriately resolve this critical issue.

Sincerely,

Jay Timmons

JT/dc

Leading Innovation. Creating Opportunity. Pursuing Progress.

733 10th Street, NW • Suite 700 • Washington, DC 20001 • P 202.637.3043 • F 202.637.3460 • www.nam.org